INTERIORS
by design

RYLAND
PETERS
& SMALL

LONDON NEW YORK

INTERIORS
by design

ADVICE AND INSPIRATION
FROM THE PROFESSIONALS

Ros Byam Shaw   *with photography by* Christopher Drake

First published in the United States in
2003 by Ryland Peters & Small, Inc.
519 Broadway, 5th Floor
New York, NY 10012
www.rylandpeters.com
This paperback edition published 2008.

10 9 8 7 6 5 4 3 2

Text © Ros Byam Shaw 2003, 2008
Design and photographs © Ryland
Peters & Small, Inc. 2003, 2008

ISBN 978 1 84597 622 4

The original edition of this book was
cataloged as follows:

Library of Congress Cataloging-in-
Publication Data
Byam Shaw, Ros.
  Interiors by design : advice and
inspiration from the professionals /
Ros Byam Shaw with photography
by Christopher Drake.
      p. cm.
Includes index.
  ISBN 1-84172-402-5
  1. Interior decoration--Handbooks,
manuals, etc. I. Drake, Christopher.
II. Title.
  NK2115.B94 2003
  747--dc21
                           2002154821

Printed and bound in China

Designer Catherine Griffin
Senior editor Clare Double
Location research Gabriella Le Grazie
Picture research Emily Westlake
Production Patricia Harrington
Art director Gabriella Le Grazie
Publishing director Alison Starling

Illustrations Marianne Topham

CONTENTS

INTRODUCTION

If you could decorate a room as quickly as you can cook a meal, you could use this like a recipe book. "That looks like a nice bedroom, I think I'll try that tonight," you could say, as you leafed through and drooled over photographs of immaculate finished rooms. Then you would have to go out and buy the ingredients, bring them home, and put them together in the same way as the professional decorator. Of course, the result would be even farther removed from the original than my pies from the perfect, golden domes of Martha's. You wouldn't be able to find all the ingredients. Your room would be a different shape. And when it was done, you wouldn't find it comfortable—it wouldn't feel like home, it would feel like someone else's room.

The truth is, there is no simple recipe for the perfect interior. The way you arrange your house should be as personal as the way you write a letter to your mother. Interiors that genuinely reflect the habits, enthusiasms, and aspirations of their inhabitants are invariably more satisfying places than ones that have been designed just for show. That being said, the very fact that you are reading this book probably means that you care about looks as well as comfort. The best rooms have both.

Innate style is rare. For the rest of us, it is a question of sticking to some of the basic rules, copying some of the ideas we like, and hoping that something approximating a style of our own will result. This book is full of beautiful rooms, and full of ideas you may be able to adapt to your own decorating purposes. It suggests things you should and shouldn't do, and reveals some of the tricks of the trade. But it can't decorate your house for you.

What I hope it will do is help you form your own ideas by giving you an insight into how the professionals form theirs. And, unlike a professional decorator, it can't present you with a bill just as your house, like Martha's pie, is done to a turn.

LEFT The bedroom of couturier Bruce Oldfield's country house fills the triangle of the steeply pitched roof. Black and white photographs of Bruce and his two foster brothers, taken in 1957, have been blown up and framed in matching wooden frames, making them look more like artworks than family snaps. THIS PICTURE Clare Mosley mixes antiques with her own creations. One of her decalcomania glass jars stands on a Georgian desk.

GETTING

STARTED

IN THE BEGINNING

Molding your own surroundings is like marking
your territory. It is something most of us feel
impelled to do even if we never get farther than a
poster and a potted plant. The strength of this urge
partly depends on how sure of our territory we are.
A temporary studio may only get the poster and
potted plant treatment but, once we are settled, the
urge becomes much stronger, and the kitchen we
inherited is likely to end up in a dumpster.

Prepare for chaos.

Decorating is time-consuming and disruptive.
Building work is worse. Any task that entails
chipping out plaster, whether you are knocking
through a doorway or simply bedding in an electric
wire, creates dust that will find its way into your
sock drawer, however many precautions you take
with plywood and parcel tape.

Enjoy your dreams.

Bearing in mind that the process will inevitably be
more or less nasty, it is worth pointing out that
getting started can be almost as pleasurable as
finishing. This is the point at which all your
decorating dreams might begin to come true, and
you find yourself endlessly musing "won't it be
lovely when…".

Accept the things you cannot change.

What is certain is that you will not be starting any
decorating project without some elements that are
already a given. Even if you were building a house
from scratch, you would be subject to building
regulations and the peculiarities of the site. As it is,
you are likely to have many more limitations,
including time, space, money, and budget, not to
mention the architectural style of your interiors and
the furnishings you already own and are fond of.

Make the best of them.
Instead of seeing these constants as limitations, you can choose to view them in a more positive light—as the framework within which to express your creativity. These are the cues that will prompt your first thoughts, the starting point for all your plans and schemes.

Be prepared to listen and to change your ideas.
Discussing your ideas with other people whose opinions you respect can be very enlightening. Of course, it is essential that all members of a household are involved in decisions that will affect them, but the advice of someone with no vested interest in your plans can often be more brave and innovative. If the person making the suggestions is not going to be the one suffering in gritty socks, they just might persuade you, quite rightly, to knock down the wall that you had decided you could live with.

Enough is enough.
There will, however, come a time when all the ruminations and kitchen table confabs must come to an end, and action must begin. But don't worry. You still need to write a brief before the dust begins to fly.

LEFT AND FAR LEFT
Looking at rooms like these, which seem so poised and perfect, it is hard to imagine they were once someone else's messy project. This particular house is characterized by neutral colors and natural materials—a good starting point for any decorating scheme.

ABOVE AND BELOW
The starting point for Angela A'Court's bathroom was the previous bathroom, which she describes as having been "very '80s." By wrapping the rolltop tub in waterproofed composite and covering it with fashionable mosaic tiles, she has brought the room up to date without breaking the bank.

The brief for this ultra-sophisticated living room would certainly have included strict specifications for the color scheme, which is particularly disciplined. Restricting the colors in a room to this range of off-whites, pale creams, and browns—the subtle, soft shades of stone and sand and wood—creates a visual environment that is soothing and easy on the eye. In this instance, it is the paintings and sculptures that mean the effect is not so easy that it is soporifically bland. Also important are the differences in texture, which are highlighted by the sameness of the colors.

CREATING A BRIEF

If you engaged a professional interior designer, your first task would be to provide them with a brief—a description of your decorating aims and ambitions, and of your aesthetic and practical requirements. As the intention of this book is to help you be your own interior designer, your first task should be to write a brief for yourself. This may sound rather contrived—why waste time writing down what you want when you already know the answers? However, as any keen list-writer will tell you, there is nothing like a pen and a piece of paper, or a computer formatted to produce bullet points, for getting jumbled thoughts in order.

Where do I start?

It is always better to live somewhere, however grotty and however drastic your plans for it, before you make irrevocable decisions. Only by inhabiting a space do you come to understand its strengths and failings and how it might best be rearranged to suit the way you live your life.

Ask yourself the sort of questions a professional would ask.

The first should probably be a decision about how much you want to spend. With that out of the way, try to look at the space you live in with a fresh, unbiased eye. Think about how you use each room, and even how you use each part of a room. If space is limited—and it usually is—what are your priorities? Would you like a bigger kitchen at the expense of your back terrace? Would you like a bigger living room at the expense of your hall? Think about storage—you can never have too much.

Keep it simple.

Fashions in interiors come and go, just as hemlines rise and fall. But it is much more expensive and disruptive to redecorate and refurnish than it is to change the contents of your wardrobe. Current fashions tend toward the plain and pared down. This is helpful for the amateur decorator since, unless you are very confident about ornament, it is less challenging to start plain and get the basics of a room right. You can always dress it up later with accessories.

Planning a room.

Work out the fundamentals of a room's use, light, heat, access, and windows; then move on to the elements within. Make a sketch plan of the available space on graph paper and cut out scale templates for key pieces of furniture so you can experiment with their positions.

Drawing up a schedule.

Now you have a better idea of what you would ideally like to achieve, you need to consider the order in which you do things. There is no point in decorating a room before you sand its floor. There is no point in sanding a floor that will have builders tramping across it to repave the back terrace. Start with wiring and plumbing and any structural changes. Move on to floors, windows, and doors. Only when these are right can you allow yourself the luxury of fabric swatches and sample paint cans.

Write everything down.

If you have a computer, use it. Otherwise, just keep making lists, crossing things out and starting again, but keep the old lists—sometimes first ideas are the best.

FINDING INSPIRATION

Inspiration is the intangible of decorating. You live in your space, you write your brief, you understand your practical needs, but still the spark that will fire you with enthusiasm for the hard work ahead is missing. Occasionally inspiration appears unbidden and as if from nowhere—a dream remembered, a sudden vision. More often, it needs prompting and prodding into life.

Look hard at what you already have.

There may be something you already own—a chair, a bedspread, a vase—that excites you visually. If it has a strong enough style and presence, you may find you can take it as your decorating cue for a whole room. Or perhaps there is something architectural about the space you inhabit, whether its style or period, which prompts visual ideas, or perhaps a single element as simple as a tiny walled backyard that could look like a Mexican courtyard, or a window that reminds you of New England.

Tear up magazines.

Buy as many decorating magazines as you can bear to and start ripping pages out if they feature anything you like the look of, from a room to a radiator. (If you can't bring yourself to vandalize expensive glossies, you will just have to buy two copies, one for ripping, one for the coffee table.) Keep a file of your clippings, ideally organized by room and theme. Decorating books can also be extremely helpful. Mark favorite pages with bits of paper sticking out and labeled "bedroom," for

ABOVE LEFT **Designer Mary Shaw finds inspiration in the colors of her native Ireland, the greens of moss and lichen, the purples of heather on distant hills. She particularly enjoys putting together similar colors woven in different fabrics and textures, like this silk throw on the back of a tweed-covered chair.**

ABOVE **Contemporary pottery in Angela A'Court's kitchen provides splashes of warm color against a background of natural wood, stone flooring, and cream walls.**

RIGHT **Comfort was the inspiration behind this huge sofa in Roger Oates' living room. Its size and the rich plum of its linen upholstery make it a visual focus as well as an invitation to curl up and relax.**

FAR RIGHT **Antique dealer Maurizio Epifani's Milan apartment is bursting with decorative objects stylish enough to inspire whole schemes, like these nineteenth-century beaded Native American moccasins.**

example, or "nice fireplace," to save you flicking through endlessly to find them again.

Be as nosy as you dare.

When you go to friends' houses, ask if you can look around—people are usually flattered rather than enraged. Take a mental note of their successes and failures. Ask them where they bought things you particularly like and write the details down for future reference.

Look to the past.

Heritage homes and other houses open to the public can also be a rich source of ideas, even if it's only the color of the corridor in the servants' quarters, or the design of a kitchen cupboard. Most large museums contain collections that concentrate on design, and they can help to get your eye in for period detail and proportion.

Nature's Bounty.

Designers often cite nature as a source of inspiration, and certainly the colors, shapes, and textures of the natural world are hard to beat. But be careful how you translate to the indoor what you love the look of outside. A riot of orange, yellow, blue, and green may look irresistibly lovely in an herbaceous bed and less delicious in your bathroom.

Know what you like.

Train yourself not to be too influenced by passing fads or by what you think will impress other people. Have confidence in your own taste. The most important thing about the style in which you decorate is that it should give you pleasure.

BELOW AND RIGHT
Cottons and linens in slightly faded colors and traditional designs are key elements of this kitchen. Vivien Lawrence found a check, a chintz, and a stripe that coordinate without looking as though they have been designed to match.

CREATING A MOOD BOARD

A mood board is a very effective way of pinning down the ideas that float around in your head and turning them into a tool you can work with. Creating a mood board will make you feel thoroughly professional at the same time as taking you on a nostalgic trip back to childhood days of collages and scrapbooks. In fact, "mood board" is just a rather grown-up name for a collage or scrapbook, but instead of using melon seeds and the most glittery Christmas cards, your aim is to gather images that evoke the colors, style, and atmosphere you would like to recreate in your decorating scheme.

Distilled inspiration.

In the previous pages, we explored ways you might find inspiration. You can't create a mood board

without an inspiration or visual idea to shape it, but once you have your finished board in front of you, it should keep that inspiration fresh and focused.

The professional mood board.

All kinds of designers use mood boards to help crystallize their ideas. A textile designer working on a line of bed linen with a seaside feel might fill a board with postcards of beach huts, snapshots of pebbles, and bits of seaweed. The finished textile may not appear to have any direct visual relationship with the images on the board, but the "mood" evoked by them will have informed its design.

The content.

Your first task is to collect pictures, textures, and colors that fit with the look you are hoping to

ABOVE **The feel of this room is relaxed and rural, with a faintly French flavor, even though the house is in a suburb a matter of miles from the center of London. A mood board for this room might have included pictures of a kitchen in a terra-cotta-floored French farmhouse, a field of lavender, a chicken coop with a wire mesh front, a basket of eggs, and a pair of shutters with flaking gray paintwork.**

THIS PAGE **Colors and textures are the basics of any mood board. Seen grouped on a page, the wobbly gloss of French pottery plates, bleached wickerwork, a creamy carpet, and a paint chart already evoke a distinctive decorative look.**

Different elements of the finished room combine to create its particular atmosphere. The country is evoked by the Windsor chairs with their rubbed paint, the old-fashioned kitchen tablecloth, and the hutch with its shelves stacked with pottery. Half-shutters at the windows, terra-cotta tiles on the floor, the curly chandelier in wood and metal, and the sun-bleached colors are responsible for the whiff of France.

achieve. Become a dedicated image hoarder for as long as it takes to gather your material. Plunder magazines, newspapers, and catalogs. Take color photocopies of pictures in books. Use scraps of material, wallpaper, ribbon, and trimming. Even small pieces of wood, cork, or metal, or leaves, flowers, or other items from the natural world, might add something in the way of tone or feel.

The practicalities.

Probably the easiest way to mount your mood board is to buy a cheap cork pinboard, at least 1½ x 2 feet in size. Now you can start to pin your photographs, postcards, ripped-out magazine pages, and other bits and pieces onto the board. You will probably find you have either too many to fit, in

which case you will have to edit your material, or not enough to fill the space, in which case you will have to continue plundering. Try to arrange the different images to make as pleasing a composition as possible. The more visually appealing your mood board, the better it will work as inspiration.

Using your mood board.

Prop your board somewhere you will see it every day, but not somewhere you will sit in front of it for hours on end, in case familiarity should breed contempt. Be prepared to add things and take things away. You might even decide you want to do something completely different after you have lived with your first attempt for a few days.

Dividing a single, large space, in this instance half of an old school auditorium, into a space for sleeping, eating, working, and relaxing, is an architectural challenge. Architect Voon Wong inserted a mezzanine floor with an open-plan office and a bedroom which is enclosed but which gains plenty of light through an internal window. The space beneath makes a dining and kitchen area, distinct from the lofty living room.

WORKING WITH SPACE

ABOVE **This huge bathroom has been carved out of windowless internal space in an attic remodel, but is flooded with borrowed light thanks to the walls of frosted glass, which enclose it on two sides. The expanse of floor between the freestanding tub and the basin and toilet on the opposite wall is a luxury in itself, but also acts as a huge shower tray, the limestone floor sloping almost imperceptibly to a central drain below a shower head that is set into the ceiling.**

To have space is a luxury. This is particularly true if you live or work in a large town or city where you spend much of your time squashed up with strangers on crowded sidewalks and buses, jostling to get served in busy stores, or fighting to keep your desk clear of other people's demands. After a day spent sharing too little territory with too many rival claimants, stepping through the door into your own space is an essential escape.

Adding space.

There are various tried and trusted ways to expand the amount of space you occupy. You may be allowed to extend your house. Most cities are full of small houses whose rooms have encroached on the backyard and along the side. If you can't extend outward, there may be scope for expanding up and making your roof space habitable with skylights and an extra flight of stairs, or ladder. However, these options are only appropriate for certain types of property and substantial budgets.

Making space.

On a more modest scale you can investigate ways of saving space, and making the space you already have

work even harder, to help your rooms feel less congested. Walk-in closets with rods one above the other (the top one can be designed to pull down for access) store twice as many clothes and take up less wall space. Washing machines and tumble dryers can stack; room dividers can double as bookshelves; drawers can be installed under beds; sliding doors disappear into the walls when open. And, if you still don't have enough space for comfort, it may be time to be more brutal with your possessions. Ask a neat, bossy friend around with some plastic trash bags and restock your local thrift store.

Creating the illusion of space.

Interior designers have probably spent as much time and effort on the problem of making spaces look bigger than they really are than on any other single design issue in recent years. Space and light are currently the most desirable qualities for an interior, and where they are not naturally abundant, there are many ways to magnify them. Mirrors and white paint are the most obvious and instantly effective space makers. All pale and receding colors open space out. Painting everything the same color, including all

woodwork, doors, and window frames, has the effect of unifying and maximizing space. A dark glossy floor gives a room depth as well as height by reflecting its contents, while using the same flooring throughout gives a sense of flow between rooms.

Going open-plan.

After years as the butt of designer derision, the open-plan interior is back. Popularized by the trend for loft-style conversions, the wide open spaces of an open-plan interior are now the height of fashion. Certainly there are many aesthetic advantages. If you take down all the internal walls, a small town house will seem remarkably spacious. However, you should think very carefully about issues of noise and privacy before you get out the sledgehammer. You may be lucky enough to have the best of both worlds; one large living area incorporating kitchen, dining, and living rooms, plus a separate study, television room, and bedrooms. If not, and you do not live alone, going open-plan can be a recipe for family discord. A less drastic solution might be to knock two rooms into one with doors between them that can be closed when necessary.

Filling your space.

Even the pokiest apartment looks relatively spacious when completely empty. Then you attempt to squeeze in your sofa, armchairs, television, sideboard, bookshelves, and coffee table, and suddenly you find you are edging around arms and legs and backs with barely space to swing a cushion. When space is limited, try to find furnishings with more than one function; a desk that can double as a dining table, a padded coffee table that can make extra seating. Always make sure there is space to move freely around a room.

Considering scale.

While it is obvious that the fewer things you have in a room, the larger it will seem, it is also worth remembering that most rooms, however small, benefit from the focus and visual clout of one large piece of furniture. Filling a small room with a lot of small pieces of furniture looks bitty and certainly won't make the room appear any larger.

Help, my room is too big.

Occasionally the problem of space is reversed, and you find yourself sitting or sleeping in a room that feels like a cavern. Again, there are various tricks you can employ. To lower a ceiling, try mounting a bold picture rail, or even plate shelf, at a more comfortable height to bring the eye down. Hanging pictures at eye level and just above has a similar effect. Screens and partition walls can be used to make rooms within rooms. Buy enormous pieces of furniture. They are often sold at a discount because so few people have enough room for them.

FAR LEFT **Once an awkward and featureless bedroom, this stylish dining room has been endowed with balance and character by the installation of plain composite paneling. There is no molding, baseboard, or beading, a strict** simplicity that makes the paneling look modern rather than like an attempt to overlay period charm. LEFT **Where there is space, two large washbasins are an extremely good use of it—the next best thing to having a bathroom each.**

THIS PAGE **Bruce Oldfield's country bathroom, like his bedroom, is tucked in the sloping eaves of the roof. Being taller than average, he has chosen a freestanding tub and placed it well away from the walls to avoid banging his head.**

COMPLETE
SCHEMES

AN ELEGANT CITY PAD

A collection of contemporary Scottish art in a London flat that brings together the old and the new with enviable panache.

ABOVE **To give architectural unity to the drawing room, which was once two rooms, a pair of matching chimney pieces in stone and steel was commissioned to face each other from either end.**
BELOW **The strong, warm colors of these William Yeoward loose-weave wool cushions, and the "Kumquat" velvet that covers the armchair, are enriched by texture.**

RIGHT **This whole room is an essay in receding and advancing color. The walls are covered in a soft duck's-egg-blue grasscloth by Bruno Triplet, chosen as a gentle, textured foil for the exuberant paintings. Equally retiring are the pale rug by Deirdre Dyson and the pair of armchairs in smoky blue linen. Only the velvet armchair and cushions compete with the paintings for the eye's attention.**

This stylish and generous apartment has benefited from a double dose of expertise. The London home of interior designer Colin Orchard and William Yeoward (who designs furniture, crystal, and other products for the home), its layout, furnishings, and architectural detailing, from chimneys to baseboards, are the product of their close collaboration.

With a second-floor view of one of London's larger parks from a series of tall windows, and windows facing south, east, and west at the back, the apartment had no shortage of light. The previous owners had already knocked down walls to make rooms bigger, doubling the size of the drawing room and incorporating a small bedroom to make a larger dining room.

Colin and William decided to go several steps further. Their reordering of the space entailed moving almost every internal wall, but the result seems so rational and right it is hard to believe it was ever any different. They moved the kitchen to the front, allowing them to group bedrooms, bathrooms, a dressing room, and small study at the back. The dining room was enlarged further and an opening knocked through into the double drawing room, which lines up directly opposite the bay window. Double doors separating the two rooms are always left open so that, even when not in use for entertaining, the dining room feels like part of the living space, rather than a room set aside and only used for special occasions.

The building dates from the late nineteenth century and its exterior is on a heritage register, so the windows could not be changed. Inside, however, all features were up for grabs. They installed new molding, extra-deep baseboards, two-panel doors, and a pair of matching chimney pieces at either end of the drawing room. The dining hall, which only has one side window, was dignified with plain painted

paneling made from composite board, to give the room what Colin calls "character and balance." In this room there are no applied moldings or baseboards, in order to keep the effect as streamlined as possible.

Throughout the apartment the flooring is wall-to-wall sisal matting, providing a consistent and neutral background. But, instead of allowing the sisal to flow through all openings, they have used a wide strip of polished oak in the doorways between the dining room and drawing room and between the drawing room and the kitchen. "Creating an illusion of space was not the most important issue," explains Colin. "The rooms are already large. The strips of wood match the wooden flooring in the entrance hall, and we wanted to create the impression that these floorboards were also under the sisal."

None of the detailing they have added is strictly "period," but nor have they taken the easier road to "modernity" by leaving the bones of the apartment bare. The impression they wanted to create was of an interior both classic and contemporary, a background for their paintings and furniture that would be clean and simple, but without its personality stripped away.

Colin and William have a talent for mixing different periods. The fluting of a Regency table and a 1930s console by Alberto Morocco (FAR LEFT) are perfectly complementary, while the dining room (RIGHT) pulls together 1940s chairs with a Yeoward dining table and modern composite paneling.

This restrained, unaffected setting is the perfect foil for their mix of possessions; furniture, fabrics, and accessories designed by William, a smattering of striking antiques, and Colin's collection of paintings by contemporary Scottish artists. The drawing room is the main gallery for the latter, and Colin chose a subtle duck's-egg-blue grasscloth against which the rich colors of the paintings seem to advance from the wall. "I wanted both color and texture for the walls," says Colin. "Texture is particularly important in this room—it gives it depth and richness. There is upholstery in velvet and rough linen, and there are cushions in a very loose-weave, tweedy wool."

The room is also notable for its bold mix of colors. Having chosen the wall color, Colin couldn't resist a chair in one of his favorite William Yeoward fabrics, a mouth-watering burnt orange velvet. "I like to keep most colors quite neutral and then splash out with the odd surprise." The orange dictated the tones of the other strong furnishing colors in the room, the three oversized sofa cushions in mustard, rust, and a particularly vibrant shade of sludge. Flowers provide further punctuations of brightness, and the paintings do the rest.

In contrast, the dining room is serene and sepia, relying for color on the dark, burnished glow of

LEFT By reconfiguring a late-nineteenth-century purpose-built flat, Colin and William created a living area with all the drama, floor space, long views, and sense of physical freedom that come with an open-plan interior. The dining room, once a poky bedroom, now opens into the double drawing room through a pair of tall doors that line up with the bay window. BELOW The colors and textures of the fabrics give the rooms a visual and tactile richness, including (1) the grasscloth on the drawing room walls, (2) the blinds, (3) the "Kumquat" velvet, and (4) the fabric used to upholster an armchair and footstool.

DOUBLE DOORS SEPARATING THE ROOMS ARE ALWAYS LEFT OPEN, SO THE DINING ROOM FEELS LIKE PART OF THE LIVING SPACE, RATHER THAN A ROOM FOR SPECIAL OCCASIONS.

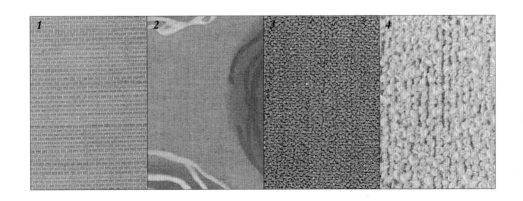

polished wood and vases of flowers at either end of the table. The furniture is not only of different periods, it is all in different types of wood; the table, a contemporary design by William Yeoward, is chestnut; the nineteenth-century Scandinavian chairs are rosewood; and the early-twentieth-century sideboard is oak. This last piece of furniture was spotted in an antique store, and pounced on for its checkerboard design, which so perfectly mirrors the paneling. Staining the oak a darker color meant it would blend with the table and chairs.

A modernist version of the dining room paneling lines the wall behind the bed in the main bedroom. The wood is chestnut, like the dining table, and is functional as well as beautiful. Behind it is the original chimney breast. Sections of the paneling open, revealing storage space in the recesses on each side for bulky items such as suitcases that don't require ready access. The paneling also acts as a built-in headboard.

The bedroom is not particularly large but space has been maximized by minimizing furnishings. Clothes storage was not necessary because there is a separate dressing room. Much of the time the sliding door, which separates the bathroom, is open, which automatically doubles the size of the room. Decorative continuity is achieved by the use in the bathroom of the same chestnut paneling to enclose the tub and partially panel the wall behind the basin. This wall has been brought forward into the room so that pipes are hidden, and there is space for useful shelving behind the mirrored doors.

The main bedroom is small but perfectly furnished with all that is required for bedtime comfort, including one of Colin Orchard's two greatest luxuries in life, down pillows (the other being a housekeeper). Sleek chestnut paneling echoes the slightly Arts and Crafts feel of the paneled dining room. But in this instance it is doing more than adding "balance and character," as it covers the chimney breast and also forms cupboard doors for storage space in the alcoves on each side. This is a particularly smart solution to the problem of providing wall space and cupboard space in one fell swoop. Although the cupboards are not immediately accessible, being behind the bedside tables, they are invaluable for keeping things like suitcases, Christmas decorations, and out-of-season clothes. The bathroom is separated by sliding doors that disappear into the walls when open, and has the same chestnut paneling surrounding the tub and behind the basin.

ABOVE **No one makes chairs and sofas quite as chaste and rigorously rectilinear as French designer Christian Liaigre. Here, his Kalfa armchairs are pushed right next to one another and lined up perfectly with a coffee table that started life as a Chinese daybed and dates back to 1800. Small gestures of color, such as the fuchsia and red cloth-covered books, and traces of pattern, such as the Miro-esque pillow** (BELOW) **are thrown into sharp relief against a background that is completely pure and plain.**

CLEAN LIVING
Sweeping away walls and replacing brick with glass turned a row house into an immaculate, modern space.

You would think there were only so many ways you could remodel a four-story, Victorian London row house to suit modern living. Yet walk through the front door of Florence Lim's house, and behind the conventional façade, you find yourself in a surprising space that is as far removed from a typical late-nineteenth-century urban interior as a Philippe Starck washbasin is from a mahogany washstand complete with flowery jug and bowl.

Instead of the usual narrow hallway, the moldings, corbels, and dado rails, cramped staircase and fussy banisters, enclosed rooms and paneled doors you might expect, you are greeted by a wide runway of pale oak floor and a long view straight through the house to a wall of glass and trees beyond. Light floods through this huge single room from front to back, and yet more light drops in from above. And there is not so much as a baseboard, let alone a fussy banister, to distract from the straight-lined purity of this uncompromisingly contemporary scene.

THIS PICTURE **Freed from distracting architectural details, this modest house has been transported into the twenty-first century, the only nineteenth-century hangers-on the glazing bars of its old sash windows. Gaining light was a priority. A conservatory built from huge slices of glass was added to the back of the house** (INSET), **giving the rear of the living room a transparent wall and a segment of glass ceiling, so that light pours in from above as well as from each end. Flooring is in wide planks of palest oak, and furnishings include such modern classics as a Barcelona daybed by Mies van der Rohe from Knoll and, at the desk, an Eames swivel chair from Vitra.**

LUXURIOUS AUSTERITY
CHARACTERIZES THE WORKING END
OF THE KITCHEN. EVERYTHING IS AS
SIMPLE AND PLAIN AS POSSIBLE.

In order to maximize the number of rooms on a small and expensive urban plot, many eighteenth- and nineteenth-century row houses dug a kitchen below sidewalk level. It didn't matter if it was dark and ill-ventilated because it was "only" inhabited by servants. Paint, glass, and some further excavation have given this semi-basement a new, and bright, lease on life.

The combination of white laminate, stainless steel, and glass gives the Bulthaup kitchen an air of clean efficiency. A glass sliding door leads from the conservatory at the rear to a small courtyard garden, which was once several feet above kitchen level and overgrown with shrubs. By bringing the level down so the cream limestone tiles continue outside, and by painting the retaining side walls of the courtyard a brilliant, light-reflecting white, the architect has recast a gloomy basement as a sunny garden room. The sinks are set in an island unit with a low glass backsplash (ABOVE), which is practical and unobtrusive. Bar stools are Spaghetti by Alias (BELOW).

When Florence Lim bought the house, it was "very, very dark and very depressing." However, she was confident that she could transform it and called on architect Voon Wong, with whom she had worked before, to help achieve her vision. Although they were not allowed to change the outward appearance of the house, the inside was gutted. They decided to leave the whole ground floor as one room with a staircase rising from it to the bedrooms on the second floor. The only telltale period details that remain are two multipane sash windows.

The light from these windows has been greatly supplemented by the addition of a glass door and a wall of glass on the back elevation, where a slim extension entirely made of glass has been added to form a modern conservatory. The glass door leads down steps into the conservatory. Next to it a piece of floor has been cut out and fenced with glass, making a skylight onto the rear of the kitchen. In this way the conservatory extension links the ground floor and basement rooms, embracing both levels and giving a second access between them.

As is so often the case in rooms that were designed for servants, the basement was particularly dark. The original kitchens and scullery were well below yard and sidewalk level, and the backyard itself was overgrown with shrubs, which cut out even more light. Voon Wong dug the backyard down almost to the level of the basement floor and painted walls and stonework bright white. The yard is still small and enclosed, but the sun bounces off the paintwork and back into the house, giving it an almost Mediterranean feel even on a gloomy winter day.

Thanks to the wall of glass with its sliding door and the light borrowed from above, the kitchen is now almost as bright a space as the living room.

Nothing in the interior has been allowed to soak up any of this precious light. The kitchen is a sleek and efficient wall of cupboards in glossy, light-reflecting white; the sofa is white, and the floor is palest limestone. Laid in large tiles that seem to expand the floor space, this limestone flows seamlessly through the conservatory extension and into the garden, linking the indoor space with the intermediary, glass-walled space and the paved courtyard beyond it. Just like the upstairs living room, this is an interior characterized by simplicity, straight lines, pale colors, and an exceptionally restrained use of ornament.

The theme continues, undiluted, in the second-floor master bedroom and bathroom. Here is the same color palette, the same extensive use of glass and natural wood, and the same restraint. In the bedroom the effect is appropriately softened by a more lavish use of fabrics. While the windows downstairs have plain Roman shades in a color of cream almost indistinguishable from the color of the paintwork, the bedroom has both shades and curtains. These are again cream, but the heavy folds of the fabric make the room seem more enclosed and cozy. Further touches of softness come from the wall-to-wall carpet, the upholstered headboard, and the addition of a large velvet cushion in a warm shade of mossy green.

Leading off the bedroom is a dressing room lined with smooth cupboards in natural wood. They contain hanging space, drawers, and shelves, and ample

THIS PAGE **The atmosphere of the house softens as you climb from the sharp clean kitchen, through the oriental simplicity of the oak-floored living room and up to the bedrooms on the second and third floors. The main bedroom feels insulated and cocooning, thanks to a carpet in a corded pale wool (1) and** thickly lined cream linen curtains. The headboard and the padded stool at its foot are upholstered in light taupe very similar in color to the upholstery of the daybed in the living room (3). The carpet continues into the dressing room, which is lined with wooden cupboards. Taupe leather (2) covers the living room's Barcelona daybed.

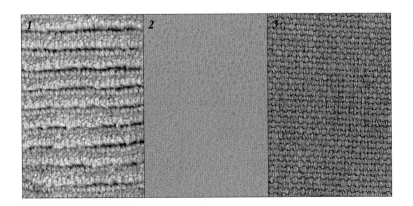

THIS PAGE **Although each floor of this cool, sophisticated home has its own particular ambience, there is decorative coherence, thanks to the repetition of materials, such as the almost-white limestone of the master bathroom (also used to floor the kitchen), and the use of glass walls, here making a perfectly** **transparent shower. Equally important is the palette of whites, creams, and taupes warmed up by the colors of natural wood, which is adhered to throughout. This bathroom is the epitome of minimalist luxury, with everything designed to eliminate visual clutter. Even the window has no blind, just frosted glass in its lower panes.**

storage to hide the clutter of clothes and shoes. And again, the lack of any carved decoration, molding, or protruding handle contributes to the sense of space.

In the bathroom we are back in the luxurious austerity that also characterizes the working end of the kitchen. Everything is kept as simple and plain as possible. The window has no blind or curtain, just lower panes in frosted glass. The shower is like a miniature version of the glass conservatory, and the limestone flooring is the same as that in the basement. Thanks to a generous central drain, there is no step into the shower, while the ceiling-mounted shower head minimizes visible pipework. In a room as streamlined as this, small visual disturbances such as half-squeezed tubes of toothpaste stick out like splashes of gravy on a starched white apron. A certain discipline is required to maintain the aura of perfect purity, and large amounts of hidden shelf space, provided in this room by the glass-fronted wall cabinet, are indispensable.

The central living room is double height with a wide galleried landing running around two sides. When Bruce Oldfield took over the house, the walls in this room were bare brick in a dark, rusty red, and the beams were dark brown. The result was a gloomy, ersatz rusticity, which was instantly banished by painting bricks and beams a soft off-white. Bruce has added to the drama of this lofty space with large-scale pieces such as the portrait of his dog and the giant pots on the table behind the sofa.

A CONVERTED MILL

Surrounded by fields and water meadows, this eighteenth-century building, once rumbling with machinery, has been transformed into a chic rural retreat by couturier Bruce Oldfield.

Imagine having a fashion designer take you in hand, look you up and down, consider your proportions, and then decide how best to dress you in order to emphasize your good points and disguise your worst. Such was the fate of this mill in Oxfordshire, which had a complete makeover by couturier Bruce Oldfield. It has been transformed from a dowdy bed and breakfast into a gloriously stylish country retreat.

Bruce Oldfield has a talent for interior design, and a proven ability to translate his eye for color and proportion from clothing bodies to dressing rooms. He has always taken a close interest in the design of his shops and has plans to expand into interior design, perhaps beginning with a small line of furniture.

When he took on the mill house, it was the setting of water meadows and fields that appealed, not the building itself. The mellow Georgian brickwork had been punctuated with replacement diamond-pane windows, and the interior had been subdivided into a warren of rooms, including serial bedrooms and bathrooms. "It isn't so much a domestic building as a country industrial building—more like a loft or a warehouse in a field," Bruce explains. "It had no particular architectural merit or any decent period features. My immediate instinct was to open it out—get rid of all the partitions, enjoy the space, and make the most of the wonderful setting by giving as many rooms as possible direct access to the outside."

ABOVE LEFT **The living room is so large that Bruce has "zoned" it by laying two big rugs in cotton-bound sisal, one marking the seating area around the fireplace, the other covering the area where there is a dining table (next to the staircase that leads down to the kitchen). The plump chaise longue is from George Smith.**
ABOVE **Bruce has an excellent eye for proportion. Even the pillows and the table lamp are big and bold, as is appropriate in a room of this scale.**

ARCHITECTURE *The kitchen is slightly below ground level, but has windows on all sides. Bruce Oldfield has not tampered with the space other than to remove later internal walls.*

MOBILE UNITS *Freestanding units in stainless steel are from Bulthaup's System 20. Some are wheeled, which gives enormous flexibility in a kitchen of this size. The fact that you can see the floor beneath them increases the room's sense of space and openness.*

WALLS *Unplastered brick walls in the kitchen and the living room are a legacy of the building's industrial origins. Bruce Oldfield has painted them off-white throughout, lightening the effect without losing their slightly rough, uneven texture.*

ACCESSORIES *Much of the atmosphere of this house comes from its close relationship with its surroundings. Fresh flowers and potted plants in every room, including the kitchen, contribute to its fresh, airy feel.*

FURNITURE *Bruce Oldfield rejected a cottage-style kitchen in favor of modernity. The high-tech glint of stainless steel makes a pleasing contrast with the old beams and diamond-pane windows and mixes equally well with the antique refectory table and chairs.*

FLOORING *A stone floor seems appropriate, both to the history of the building and to the room's more recent incarnation as a country kitchen, while the distinctive variegated colors of the Indian slate give it a slightly exotic twist.*

Only a person as neat and aesthetically disciplined as Bruce Oldfield can afford to have so much on display. Just as he stores clothing, perfectly folded on open shelves in the bedroom, in the kitchen everyday items, whether assorted flatware or serving plates and casserole dishes (RIGHT), are laid out for all to see, while glasses are stored in a transparent medical cabinet. The wood, pottery, and old bone-handled knives (LEFT) fit perfectly with the rustic sophistication of this eminently practical room.

Opening out became the decorative theme of the whole house, which now has many fewer bedrooms but a spectacular sense of space. The main living room, which has a door leading through to the garden and a French door giving onto a decking balcony over the millrace, is double height up to the beamed roof. This gives the room the exhilarating volume of a church or an ancient barn. A simple gallery of white-painted banisters runs around two sides of the room, allowing space for an open-plan library, a tempting place to sit and read while surveying the view below.

The room is so big that Bruce has divided it into zones. Helping to mark them are two large, bound sisal mats laid over the floorboards. One of these stretches across in front of the fireplace, where a sofa and armchairs invite relaxed conversation. The other covers the second half of the room, where there is a dining table draped in a linen cloth, next to the stairs leading down to the kitchen.

The sense of openness is enhanced by the furnishings, which are large and few. A huge sketch of Bruce's beloved Rhodesian Ridgeback hangs over the fireplace. Propped to its right is a tall mirror, which reflects the windows in a long enfilade of light. A pair of giant china pots holds small trees on the table behind the sofa, and even the cushions are extra big. Walls and woodwork are white and off-white, making the most of the abundant daylight. Warmer color in shades of burnt orange, mustard, and the glossy browns of antique wood build up a scheme that is gentle and welcoming, as well as bright.

By knocking out further walls Bruce made a kitchen, which fills the whole ground floor with windows on every side and views of leafy pots. Instead of opting for a rustic look Bruce chose a freestanding modular kitchen by Bulthaup. "I like the

RIGHT The original stable-style back door opens straight into the kitchen, where one of the Bulthaup mobile kitchen units has been wheeled next to the sink. The collision of old-fashioned country style—metal latches, roughly carved beams, Wellington boots—with the sharp contemporary design of the kitchen cupboards and drawers works particularly well in this building which, although rural, also retains an industrial edge.

clash of its slightly industrial, modern looks with the country feel of the beams and windows," he comments, "and I also like the fact that you can see a dead mouse under the units." In addition to allowing views of dead mice, the space beneath the kitchen units and the predominance of open shelving maximize the view of the new slate floor and make the room seem even more expansive. A restored medical cabinet with glass doors and shelves makes a cleverly transparent divider between kitchen and stairs and continues the theme of openness.

At the top of the house the main bedroom and bathroom are squeezed into the triangle of the roof, a potentially uncomfortable arrangement for a man of Bruce's stature. Bathtub and bed had to be placed away from the walls, to give enough ceiling height. The tub, like the kitchen units, is freestanding, and the bed is anchored in the middle of the room by a set of sturdy shelves that double as clothes storage and headboard. Clothes are beautifully folded, just as pans in the kitchen are neatly stacked. And, again, space is magnified.

OPENING OUT BECAME THE DECORATIVE THEME OF THE WHOLE HOUSE, WHICH NOW HAS FEWER BEDROOMS BUT A SPECTACULAR SENSE OF SPACE.

ABOVE **Tucked into the steep pitch of the roof, the bathroom and bedroom have the extra rustic feel of a barn. The slope of the ceiling gives the rooms immense character, but is far from practical.**
RIGHT **The room is large, if awkwardly shaped, allowing enough space for that ultimate bathroom luxury, a sofa. A corded wool carpet covers this end of the room while the bathtub stands on a raised platform of wooden boards, allowing space for the plumbing beneath.**

The only comfortable place for a bed in a room this shape is in the middle. But a central bed can feel unpleasantly exposed. Bruce Oldfield has addressed the problem by designing a chunky set of open shelves in untreated wood. They serve the dual purpose of providing a solid and protective headboard, and taking the place of bedside tables, which would be a nuisance in this particular layout. They are also open storage for Bruce's perfectly folded, beautifully coordinated clothes.

THE ROOMS

LIVING ROOMS

The modern living room is a hard-working space. Unlike the genteel drawing room of the past, where ladies withdrew after dinner, or the parlor kept pristine for best, today's main reception room is used and lived in, just as its new name suggests. This is where we relax in company or as a family, where we gather around the fire or in front of the television. It may also be the room where we work at a computer, get lost in a book, or wade through the Sunday papers over a prolonged cup of coffee. But despite the informality of the twenty-first-century home, the living room is still the room where we are most at pains to display our personal style. More than private retreat, it is also the most public face of our home. Combining the elegance of formality with the comfort of informality is a trick all these designers have learned to master.

FORMAL INVITATION Symmetry and discipline inform the layout and palette of this apartment in central Milan. Home of interior designer Daniela Micol Wajskol, it epitomizes her style, mixing classical proportions with homespun simplicity for an elegant blend of comfort and formality.

LEFT The apartment is grandly proportioned, with floor-to-ceiling windows, many of which open onto small balconies. Daniela has echoed the architectural formality of the drawing room by arranging furnishings to balance one another on each side of the fireplace and, in the case of the pots and lamps on the mantelpiece (BELOW RIGHT) and the antique drawings on either side, by arranging them with perfect symmetry. However, there are also elements of the interior design that work against this formality, such as the simple curtains, the slightly crumpled linen upholstery, and the rubbed and distressed paintwork of some of the furniture. RIGHT Abundant Italian sunlight is spread into the hall, loosely divided from the drawing room by pillars, and the dining room, which is separated by glass doors and internal windows (BELOW LEFT).

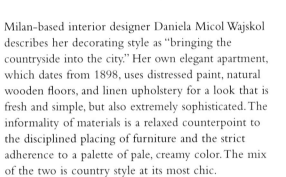

Milan-based interior designer Daniela Micol Wajskol describes her decorating style as "bringing the countryside into the city." Her own elegant apartment, which dates from 1898, uses distressed paint, natural wooden floors, and linen upholstery for a look that is fresh and simple, but also extremely sophisticated. The informality of materials is a relaxed counterpoint to the disciplined placing of furniture and the strict adherence to a palette of pale, creamy color. The mix of the two is country style at its most chic.

The apartment already had high ceilings, tall windows, and a degree of architectural symmetry, plus "a magical atmosphere" that Daniela was at pains to preserve. Her approach as interior decorator was to enhance what was already there. Light floods in from the high casement windows of the drawing

room and flows through into the hall, from which it is loosely divided by two pillars. Internal windows and glazed doors separate the dining room. The absence of solid walls between these three rooms not only means that all benefit from maximum daylight, it also gives long vistas between them, making the most of the generous floor space.

Small touches of color differentiate these three almost open-plan spaces; the dining room has pretty pink toile de Jouy upholstery on the chairs, the hall has a carpet in very dark blue and gold. But the colors in the living room hardly veer from the whites, golds, and browns that ripple in the marble of the chimney. Linking them all is the soft white of walls and woodwork.

The colors in themselves are visually soothing, melting into one another. The only strong contrasts are provided by the fireplace with its deep black interior and the slim black speakers flanking it. In winter the fire is lit, but in summer it remains a focus for the room, not only because the sofa, daybed, and

CURTAINS *Instead of aggrandizing the room with the swags and drapes that might be thought appropriate to windows of this stature, Daniela chose the plainest curtain treatment in a simple cotton-linen check for an injection of fresh informality.*

PICTURES *These are hung low, another decorative ploy to deflate the grandeur of this high-ceilinged room. The set of four antique architectural drawings has been framed by moldings applied to the wall, reinforcing the effect of lowering the ceiling.*

WALLS *The hall, living room, and dining room are united by a warm off-white paint the color of heavy cream, which has also been used on all the woodwork, windows, and moldings, as well as on the ceiling.*

FLOORING *It is an Italian decorative tradition to eschew the comfort of soft flooring in favor of the crisp beauty of wood, stone, or terrazzo. Daniela has left the polished oak boards in the living and dining rooms bare of rugs.*

TEXTILES *The sofa, daybed, and pair of armchairs are upholstered in a creamy, slightly rough textured linen. The daybed is a classical design made less formal by the addition of a plumply padded squab cushion.*

ARCHITECTURE *The volumes and windows were beautiful, then Daniela opened up the space by knocking three tall arches between the hall and living room. Adding paneling and molding to the remaining wall has given them the structural dignity of pillars.*

chairs are arranged around it, but because the eye is pulled toward its black rectangle, so sharply framed by the white marble.

Daniela has made the most of the apartment's classical proportions by arranging pictures, furniture, and ornaments with a strong bias toward symmetry. Again, the status of the fireplace as focus of the room is emphasized by the perfect balance of the arrangement on the mantelpiece and the pictures on each side. Daniela added an extra frame of wall paneling to surround these architectural prints and chose to hang them deliberately low. Furnishings are also consistently low—there are no tall cupboards or towering bookshelves, and there is no hanging lighting. This has the effect of making the room seem more informal than it might otherwise.

The success of this room is as much a result of what has been omitted as what has been included. It takes a strict vision, for example, to leave a polished wooden floor completely bare of rugs. But Daniela has chosen to do just that in the living room and adjoining dining room. The beautiful oak boards are free from visual clutter, and the rooms seem bigger and less encumbered as a result, as if you could just push the furniture aside and hold a dance. And the plump upholstery of the sofa with its giant cushions and the daybed with its squashy mattress look all the more inviting.

ABOVE **An aristocratic chaise longue, set aside from the main seating area in the living room, has its own attendant lamp, making an inviting place for a quiet read. Behind it are the internal windows and pair of glass doors that separate the dining room, (CENTER). Whether these doors are open or shut, the glass allows a view from each room into the other, and increases the sense of space and the flow of light.**
BELOW RIGHT **Swatches of the simple, even humble, fabrics used in these rooms include (1) the pale sand cotton of the cushion covers, (2) and (3) the shades of pale oatmeal in different linen weaves used on the sofa and chaise longue and (4) the green and ginger check on cream of the curtain fabric.**

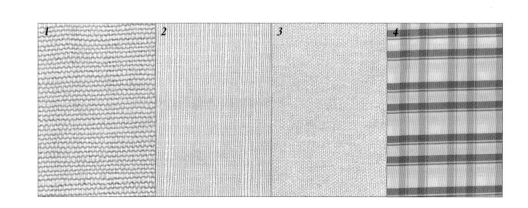

Designers can never resist making changes in their own homes, and Roger Oates and Fay Morgan are no exception. What has not changed is a characteristic simplicity enlivened by their sure eye for color and attention to texture.

A CONSTANTLY CHANGING SPACE

Last time I wrote about this living room, it had quite a different feel. Walls were painted in panels of deep strawberry, there were heavy linen curtains, and there was more furniture. It now has a mix of modern furniture and a couple of simple, antique pieces, which look as effective as ever in this period setting of paneled doors, sash windows, and fireplace. The room belongs to designers Roger Oates and Fay Morgan, who are probably best known for their line of natural floor coverings, flatweave rugs, and stair runners. It fills one side, from front to back, of the ground floor of their double-fronted Georgian country house.

The walls and woodwork have been repainted pale shades of stone and sand, and all traces of strawberry are banished. There is color, but it is soft and gentle; the rich plum of the linen covering the sofa; brown, mustard, and gray cushions; and the subtle mossy green of the felted floor mat. The remainder of the palette relies on the many shades of natural wood, from the honey brown of the old stripped-pine doors to the bleached grain of the Christian Liaigre stools.

Contributing to the light, airy atmosphere are the iridescent, semisheer curtains, attached by clips to a slim stainless-steel pole. These offer a degree of privacy at the front of the house, which looks onto the street, but would not be adequate without the original shutters, which pull up from shutter boxes below the sash windows. The combination of shutters with light, plain curtains has a modern simplicity while respecting and even highlighting the old, paneled woodwork and fine grid of the Georgian glazing bars.

This double room was once two rooms, so it divides quite obviously into a sitting and a dining end.

FAR LEFT The plain fielded paneling of the original Georgian doors, now stripped back to the bare wood, finds an echo in the straight lines and right angles of a contemporary chair. This is the type of visual link that allows old and new to coexist and complement one another.
CENTER LEFT Softening the spindles of an Arts and Crafts sofa are pillows in yellow and purple, complementary colors toned down to earthy mustard and dusky damson.
LEFT A pair of stools in untreated wood by Christian Liaigre sits on the Roger Oates felted wool rug. The materials have a timeless quality, but the design is distinctly contemporary.
BELOW FAR LEFT AND THIS PAGE Placed next to each other, you can see how well the colors and textures of the fabrics used in this room work together. The thick green felted wool (1) is the carpet, the damson linen (2) covers the large sofa and cushions on the wooden sofa, and the burnt orange linen (3) and marled brown linen-cotton mix (4) also cover cushions. Paintwork throughout is Farrow & Ball Old White.

There are two sofas at the sitting end, one an original Arts and Crafts piece, square and upright, its spindles softened by pillows. This is not, however, a sofa for lounging. For that there is a new sofa, "so big a giant could sleep on it," Fay says. Aside from comfort, the room needed "grounding" with one really large piece of furniture. Balancing the bulk of this sofa, there is a large table at the other end of the room. Its white laminate top gives it a clean look and matches the pure white linen slipcovers over the dining chairs. The console is used for serving dinner-party food.

One of the charms of this room is the impression it gives of flexibility and decorative freedom; the trestle table can be dismantled if space is needed, pictures are propped rather than hung, and slipcovers can be whipped off without having to undo a button. "I like a room to be beautiful, functional, and uncluttered," Fay states. "You should have the ability to move furniture around, and to move around the furniture." To this end, Fay and Roger have a whole room in their house given over to storage, where they keep things they do not want to give away but which are surplus to the current scheme. Fay is also brutal about things she doesn't like and hates what she calls "small bits." Ornaments are few and simple, and the result looks both graphic and sophisticated.

Sometimes the layout of a period house converts very neatly to the demands of modern life. This house would once have had two rooms on each side of the staircase hall. On the right-hand side they have been knocked into one, making it easy to divide the space into living and dining areas. It is interesting to note how well the plain contemporary furnishings fit with the plain eighteenth-century architecture. Because this would not have been a particularly grand house, detailing is minimal, although the rooms and windows are well proportioned. The original chimneys had been replaced, and one has been blocked in at this end of the room to release more wall space and make a place for the piano.

It somehow looks as though it should be easy to create a room this dramatic. The furnishings are few, and the color scheme as bold as a child's drawing of a fire engine. In fact, its success relies on close attention to line and proportion and a sophisticated balancing of bold blocks of color. The horizontal rectangles of the Charles sofas by Citterio, and the dark oblong of the fireplace, have vertical counterparts in the tall sliding panels on each side of the chimney breast, which are painted in shades of charcoal and pale gray. The dominance of the straight line is relieved by the curve of the lamp, the CVO Firevault fire bowl, and the chaise; the flat textures of leather and wool by the shaggy rug; and the plain colors by the busy detail of the Jack Milroy artwork. BELOW RIGHT More sculpture than seating, the chaise by Poul Kjaerholm.

REMODELING 1960S STYLE
Disguised beneath genteel and entirely bogus additions lurked a lost piece of modernist architecture. Fiona McLean uncovered, and dressed, its clean lines.

Most architects and interior designers have had plenty of practice when it comes to reinstating period details in old houses, features that were stripped away in the 1950s and 1960s when flush doors and boxed-in banisters were all the rage. For this house, surrounded by garden and overlooking a golf course on the edge of London, the process was reversed.

Built in the 1960s with the stern, boxy aesthetic of a two-story office building, the house was prettified twenty years later with the addition of a mansard roof, windows with glazing bars, and louvered shutters. The effect, says architect Fiona McLean, was like a suburban parody of a French chateau.

When called in by her clients to remodel the house, Fiona's first task was to restore the clean lines of the original. Out went the wooden windows and glazing bars, to be replaced by metal-framed picture windows. In the second-floor living room, an ornate marble fireplace, baseboards, and moldings were all disposed of. Tall, metal-framed French (as opposed to Frenchified) doors were installed, and the fireplace was returned to its former stark geometry.

The house had originally been designed with limestone flooring on the ground floor. Fiona decided to reinstate it, and also to use it for the living room, where it appears to slip beneath the windows and sliding doors to pave the roof terrace.

Fiona's scheme is more than a straightforward restoration, to the extent that she has made her own

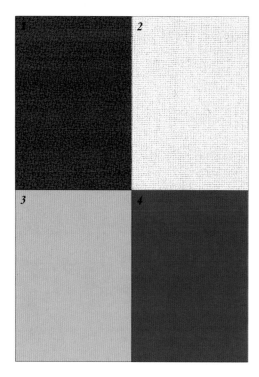

architectural additions. In the corners of the living
room, on each side of the chimney breast, she cut
two tall slot windows, shielded by sliding shutters,
which allow a view from front to back of the house.
She also decided that the proportions of the room
would be better if the ceiling were lowered to line
up with the top of the windows. This allowed her to
create a suspended ceiling, which appears to float,
framed by a shadow gap, which she likes to think of
as the "modern equivalent of a cornice."

Walls and ceiling are painted white except for the
fireplace and alcoves on each side, which are in her
favorite charcoal gray. "It's the color of shadow," she
explains, "and gives a sense of tremendous depth."
Pure white Roman shades soften the light. Into this
pristine space Fiona planted two brave slabs of color.
"The view from the windows was so green that its
complementary color seemed to balance it."

The primary red of the sofas also warms what
might otherwise be a rather cool interior. The thick,
tactile rug does the same, as well as helping to absorb
sound and soften the acoustics. A fascinating three-
dimensional artwork by Jack Milroy picks up on
both color and texture, and draws the eye with its
intricacy in a room of studied simplicity.

The comfort offered by these furnishings contrasts
with the formality of their arrangement. The pair of
sofas, the coffee table, and the leather upholstered
bench present a symmetrical series of straight lines
and right angles, perfectly aligned with the rectangles
of the chimney breast. The swoop of the Arco floor
lamp and the curves of the chaise longue and the fire
bowl offer a kind of visual relief and counterpoint.
And, like the colors, a satisfying balance is achieved.

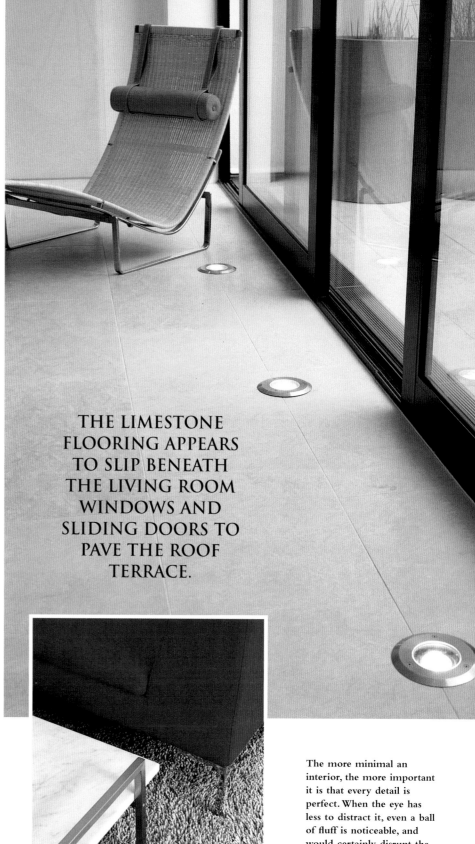

THE LIMESTONE
FLOORING APPEARS
TO SLIP BENEATH
THE LIVING ROOM
WINDOWS AND
SLIDING DOORS TO
PAVE THE ROOF
TERRACE.

The more minimal an
interior, the more important
it is that every detail is
perfect. When the eye has
less to distract it, even a ball
of fluff is noticeable, and
would certainly disrupt the
serenity of the flawless
limestone that sweeps from
the indoors out (ABOVE).
Contrasts become more
pointed, here between the
red wool of the sofas (1),
the pristine white cotton of
the shades (2), and the gray
paints by Akzo Nobel used
each side of the chimney
breast (3 and 4). Texture is
equally telling (LEFT).

The eye takes pleasure in difference, and here it has plenty to feast on, even though furnishings are sparse and decorative flourishes a rarity. The Arco floor lamp by Castiglione, a classic of 1960s design, exerts a strong visual pull, being large scale, curving in a room dominated by right angles, and shiny, while Jack Milroy's artwork, which consists of hundreds of pages pierced by cut-out fish and encased in Perspex, is like a static version of an aquarium and just as fascinating to look at.

RIGHT **The thing that first strikes you about this room is the rainbow of colors it encompasses; shades of green, orange, purple, yellow, and pink. In fact, there are two quite different color schemes, or "ambiences," as Mary Shaw calls them. The dining end of the room is a rich, dark pudding, with damson linen curtains sinking to a deep border of dusky green velvet, purple walls above a lichen-green dado, and chairs tightly covered in heathery tweeds (LEFT). If these are the rich shades of twilight, the living end of the room is a summer afternoon glowing with gold, saffron, and mustard (FAR LEFT AND BELOW). The buttonback chair in coppery tweed is placed where the two color schemes meet to act as a "transitional" shade. Finding a color that is equally at home in two contrasting schemes is Mary's tip for making a visual link between them and achieving an overall harmony.**

CREATIVE COLOR **There is something delicious about the way Mary Shaw mixes colors. From "plum" to "wheat," they sound good enough to eat.**

Mary Shaw's Paris showroom epitomizes the way she likes to live. Comfortable, elegant, glowing with color, it mixes styles and periods with wit and courage, for a result that is entirely harmonious.

When Mary Shaw established her design business, Sequana, in 1997, she wanted to draw on the wealth of traditional skills and craftsmanship in rural France and her native Ireland, and bring their products up to date by using them in a contemporary way. Woven tweeds from Ireland and Scotland gain an element of surprise when used to make cushions instead of knickers or deerstalkers. Plain linens dyed exotic colors and mixed with velvet make chic curtains. A Napoleon III chair upholstered in herringbone wool guarantees you look afresh at both chair and fabric.

Mary Shaw has a particular talent for intriguing juxtapositions. The apartment is classic Parisian, dating from about 1900, with eighteenth-century-style paneling, marble chimney pieces, floor-to-ceiling windows, and honey-colored oak parquet. Instead of furnishing it in classic Parisian style, with rubbed gilt, slim-legged antiques and pale, dusty colors, Mary Shaw has filled these light, bright rooms with abstract paintings, huge black and white photographs, plump old armchairs tightly clothed in a rainbow of tweeds, and modern stools and daybeds

LEFT The colors of the checked tweed wool on the antique chair unite all the different shades of paintwork, curtains, and even the honey brown of the parquet flooring, at the dining end of the living room. Handmade glasses, as glossy as hard candy, are in the same color range, and the metal table has an enameled top, again in rich, jewellike colors. The curtains at this end of the room are heavily lined in accordance with its more cozy and enclosed atmosphere, while the curtains at the windows of the living room are a layer of unlined linen with an overlay of wafting linen voile attached at the top.

ABOVE AND INSET LEFT A sofa at one end of the room is a cornucopia of texture and soft color; herringbone tweed throws are edged with smooth linen or made into a patchwork, and even the cushion buttons are covered with matching tweed.
ABOVE RIGHT Throws in silky mohair introduce yet another texture in a room full of fabrics and surfaces you feel drawn to touch.
RIGHT A selection of Mary Shaw's colorful tweeds, each one subtly flecked.

made to her own design. Also her design are the tall, metal floor lamps. Pottery and glass is specially commissioned from craftsmen and designer-makers.

Rather than a decorator, Mary Shaw describes herself as someone who "puts ambiences together." The salon of this graceful apartment illustrates perfectly what she means. Glazed doors divide the space into a living and dining end, each of which has a very different feel. Yellows, ambers, and golds predominate in the living room, where the walls are painted a soft, deep shade that Mary has christened "straw." In the same sunshine palette the curtains are two layers of linen joined at the top, one a heavier weave in a gentle shade of gold with, over it, a layer of diaphanous linen voile with a cream warp and a golden weft. Even when the sky is gray, this room feels as though it is flooded with sunlight.

The doors between the rooms are usually open, and the dining room, with its plum-red walls and thick heavy curtains in damson linen and deep green velvet, is in strong contrast, a nighttime room that feels enclosed and cozy. Mary Shaw likes strong color contrasts, but knows how to avoid jarring the eye. "I used the copper-colored armchair that sits between the rooms to provide a transitional shade, which links the two color schemes," she explains.

Mary successfully mixes many different colors in a single room by choosing a range of shades that are close to one another, like orange, red, and yellow, or complementary, like green and purple. The sunny side of her sitting room features the warm oranges, ambers, browns, and reds of fall leaves, while the darker, dining end is inspired by the colors of the Irish landscape where she grew up, lichen greens and the purples of heather and distant mountains. None of the colors she uses is pure. The tweeds, for example, when looked at closely, contain flecks of many different shades. As a result, no one color predominates, and the overall effect is gentle.

LEFT **One of the quickest ways to make a room seem larger and brighter is to replace curtains with minimal shades or, as in this case, shutters. This room had heavy curtains at two sash windows, one French door, and a large bay window, with the result that it felt too enclosed.**

COUNTRY FASHION

Country furniture from France and Sweden, seagrass matting, and gingham upholstery in a London living room that is relaxed, informal, and pretty.

The brief for this living room was to make it seem larger and lighter, and to give it a simple, fresh, country feel. Interior designer Vivien Lawrence took up the challenge. "The room already had many advantages," she explains. "The house was built at the beginning of the last century by architects Unwin and Parker in one of the new garden suburbs and is surrounded by its own garden on three sides. Every room, including this, has double, or triple aspects. So, although it isn't a particularly large room, it had all the potential to be bright and airy, with French doors leading onto a terrace and a beautiful bay window opposite."

The first change Vivien made was to remove the heavy curtains that hung at all three windows. "They made the room very cozy at night, but during the day it felt too enclosed and suffocating." Vivien replaced the curtains with shutters, which fit neatly into the window recesses on the window to the right of the fireplace and by the French doors. When open, they are barely noticeable, and when shut, their plain panels fit well with the Queen Anne revival style of the interior architecture.

Shutters could not be made to fit the bay window. In order to achieve uniformity, Vivien used false shutters, and hung cream London blinds for privacy. This plain window treatment adds softness with minimal visual clutter. The blinds are also performing a less obvious role by improving the proportions of the bay window, which is actually much lower than the other two windows. While the blinds appear to be covering the top of the window, they are in fact masking the wall above. The effect is to make it seem as if all the windows in the room reach nearly to ceiling height.

ABOVE **The pale paintwork of this French provincial corner cupboard finds an echo in the cream-on-cream stripes of the wall. The marble-topped side table with its charming curves is another French antique.**

OPPOSITE BELOW **Delicate decorative touches such as this embroidered pillow give the room a distinctly feminine aura.**
BELOW **A loose arrangement of ornaments is chic in shades of white.**

SHADES *These simple, white Roman shades cleverly disguise the fact that the top of the bay window is lower than the rest of the windows in the room. The false shutters were added for the sake of decorative unity.*

WALLS *The walls have been painted with thick stripes in darker cream on paler cream. Their width gives them gentle impact, and because they reach right up to ceiling level they make the room seem taller.*

PICTURES *These are few but quite dramatic—large oils in old gilt frames. Each is also framed by its own piece of wall with plenty of empty wall space around it, allowing the room to breathe.*

TEXTILES *The pair of sofas is upholstered in cream linen with cushions in a slubby cream silk and an embroidered cushion as a centerpiece. The bold check of the pale blue gingham on the armchair introduces soft color and country-cottage simplicity.*

FLOORING *Seagrass matting is chic but also rustic. Its undyed color and woven texture make it seem more natural than carpet, and its sweet scent, like fresh hay, lasts for years after it is first laid.*

ACCESSORIES *Ornaments are few, and pretty, like this rosebud-scattered lamp base. Silver and glass predominate, with an emphasis on the feminine and a bias toward the antique.*

LEFT AND BELOW RIGHT
The materials and finishes
in any room are as
important to its overall
effect as the furniture.
Much of the fresh, airy
country feel in this room
derives from the emphasis
on natural materials, the
unbleached heavy silk that
covers the cushions (1), the
cream linen of the sofas (2),
and the blue and cream
gingham of the armchair
(3). Combine these with
seagrass matting, a hand-
painted wall in a classical
stripe, fabric furnishings in
traditional shapes, and the
rubbed white paintwork of
an antique provincial
secretaire and you have the
ingredients for an informal
and slightly rustic flavor.
RIGHT The black and
white photographs in silver
and *verre eglomise* frames
add a personal touch while
remaining true to the
old-fashioned elegance
of the room.

THE FRESH COUNTRY FEEL COMES COURTESY OF WALL-TO-WALL SEAGRASS AND BLUE AND WHITE CHECK UPHOLSTERY.

The color scheme of the room is based around shades of cream. Walls and woodwork are painted off-white. But rather than leave the walls plain, Vivien decided to overlay them with wide painted stripes in a slightly darker shade of cream. The result is classical without being grand, and the gentle uninterrupted verticals rising from baseboard to molding make the ceiling appear higher, again increasing the sense of volume in the room.

Pale colors and windows free of curtains and valances immediately doubled the amount of light. The next task was to pare furniture down to the essentials to liberate as much floor space as possible. Two pieces of the painted provincial furniture the client collects found their natural place; the antique

Swedish secretaire and the old French corner cabinet. Twin sofas face one another across the fireplace, and a large coffee table was replaced by a smaller, more delicate piece with a glass top. Additional seating is provided by the armchair and the padded window seat. Vivien also removed pictures, allowing the walls space to breathe. "Comfortable seating and somewhere to put your drink is all you really need," she says.

As for the last element of the brief, the "fresh country feel" comes courtesy of wall-to-wall seagrass, the innocent blue and white check of upholstery, the rubbed paintwork of the desk and cupboard, and small, but telling, details like the flower-embroidered pillow and the informal mantelpiece arrangement.

RED ALERT

Be careful, says John Barman, with powerful primaries—they are demanding and difficult. His own Manhattan apartment, which uses lashings of bright red, shows how a dangerous color can make a handsome interior.

Red is American interior designer John Barman's favorite color. Not just any red. Bright, bold, fire engine red, a shade to set your pulse racing. In his own twenty-first floor Manhattan apartment, Barman has indulged himself with red in spadefuls. The huge living room, with its three walls of window, features five chairs upholstered in bright red, including a pair of Mies van der Rohe Barcelona chairs in sleek buttoned leather, a bright red glass ashtray, and a large bright red textured rug.

"I find red exciting to live with," says Barman, but he also warns that it is difficult to put other colors with this particular shade of red. Not that he doesn't enjoy other colors; his bedroom, for example, is yellow. But with a scheme that uses a pure primary shade as powerful as red, you need to be very careful what you mix in with it. Barman's advice is simple. "Stick to your point of view." And, if this point of view happens to be a love of red, then stick to a tried and trusted formula, and match it with black and white. The result is uncompromising and incredibly stylish, like the most glamorous soldiers' uniforms.

Although these colors are the perfect complement to one another, care still needs to be taken to balance them. Barman uses white as his background color and a fairly even distribution of black and red between the various furnishings. His scheme is greatly enhanced by the sculptural forms of the twentieth-century classics he collects: each piece of furniture makes a bold statement with its strong lines and lack of surface decoration; there are no fancy moldings, applied decorations, frills, or fringes to distract from the purity of color and form. Built in the 1980s, the apartment is also architecturally plain, without so much as a molding or baseboard. By leaving the walls free of pictures and the ceiling free of light fixtures, Barman provides as pure and uncluttered a background as possible for his cast of three-tone furnishings.

Even with perfect balance, such a limited palette could be visually tiring. Again this room succeeds because any potential monotony of tone is relieved by striking contrasts of texture. Red leather chairs sit on a red rug, but the leather is smooth with a slight sheen while the rug is deeply tufted, its softness emphasized by a pattern of raised squares, which form a geometric bas-relief. The black upholstery is woven wool and darkest gray velour; the white curtains are diaphanous and fall in gentle folds. And then there are the shiny surfaces; the soft gloss of the polished concrete floor, the glint of the shiny metal chair frames, and the reflective smoked glass of the coffee table. Most theatrical of all is the 1970s mirrored screen. Like a space-age version of the old-fashioned convex butler's mirror, its surface reflects multiple views of the room and its occupants, distorted and refracted in a series of mobile vignettes.

This is a room of extreme drama that some would find hard to live with, or up to. But it is also a fine example of how three strong colors, applied with style and discipline, can be corraled to make an interior of distinction and originality.

The setting and sheer volume of the apartment are dramatic enough; twenty-one floors up with a huge living area of 30 x 25 feet and views through three walls of window of soaring buildings and slices of sky. Architecturally the space is featureless. Barman has painted walls and ceiling brilliant white and has used bright white sheer curtains, which barely impinge visually. Into this box of light he has introduced classic pieces of twentieth-century furniture, a few pieces of ornamental ceramic and glass, and a color scheme of red, white, black, and gray that is absolutely strict. The effect is disconcertingly sci-fi—like an interior from the Starship Enterprise—but also comfortable, thanks to the thick rug, the capacious sofa, and the welcoming curves of armchairs.

Barman balances color with an artist's eye, juggling blocks of red and black against his plain white background. But he has paid equal attention to differences in texture and to the impact of line. Both are important in the context of a color scheme that offers such bold contrasts.

THIS PAGE Even though it is pure white, the curves of the Eero Saarinen table have an impact in a room where each piece is given space and status, while the bow of the metal chair arms is etched against the walls.

OPPOSITE Extremes of texture are just as pointed as the contrasts in color. Here the shiny, reflective surfaces of the 1970s mirrored screen and the smoked glass coffee table meet their opposites in the shadowy gray velour of the chairs.

MOST THEATRICAL OF ALL IS THE 1970S MIRRORED SCREEN, LIKE A SPACE-AGE VERSION OF THE OLD-FASHIONED CONVEX BUTLER'S MIRROR.

LEFT David Mullman reorganized the layout, allowing space and light to flow more freely between rooms by opening up large doorways and internal windows. The tall triple window, which lights the living and dining rooms, is one of the few architectural features left from the original 1925 design. The apartment is on the eighth floor facing a fifteen-story building, so the outlook is "nothing special." Curtains are two layers of linen scrim. One layer is in cream and screens the view during the day; the other is mocha brown and can be pulled across for privacy at night.

COFFEE AND CREAM

Vanilla ice-cream and dark chocolate would do equally well to describe the delectable colors in this New York apartment, recently remodeled and brought up to date by David Mullman.

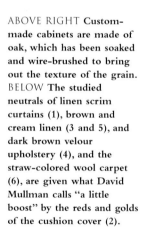

ABOVE RIGHT Custom-made cabinets are made of oak, which has been soaked and wire-brushed to bring out the texture of the grain. BELOW The studied neutrals of linen scrim curtains (1), brown and cream linen (3 and 5), and dark brown velour upholstery (4), and the straw-colored wool carpet (6), are given what David Mullman calls "a little boost" by the reds and golds of the cushion cover (2).

Apartments in New York City are commonly divided into the prewar and the postwar, a description that refers as much to their construction as their style. The former, says architect and interior designer David Mullman, are less problematic to renovate because, unlike the latter, they are not built of solid slabs of concrete. Internal walls can be moved more easily and the layout of rooms reorganized.

This sharp, modern living room, with its flat planes and straight lines, has been created in a prewar apartment, dating from about 1925. The owners wanted a clean, contemporary look, so David's first task, as he puts it, was to "iron out" all the corners.

Ornate moldings were replaced with a simple box cornice, which continues in front of the windows to make a valance for the curtains, while the pillars, which once gave the room an ersatz classical grandeur, were encased in the wall, which now divides the living and dining areas.

Going open-plan was not a structural option.

Instead David Mullman created extra large openings between the rooms. The doorway is eight feet tall by six feet wide, and the window as wide. These openings are also deep, partly because they are wrapped around the original pillars. Their depth is emphasized by the dark wood lining them. David Mullman likes this effect of very thick walls. "It gives the apartment more heft, more substance and more strength," he says.

One of the original features they retained was the flooring, a dark stained oak. Polished and treated to bring out the grain, its rich chocolate gloss dictated the palette of colors for walls and furnishings. "Initially the clients wanted to keep all the colors very neutral—off-whites, beige, straw, and taupe, but we persuaded them that the room needed the boost of some warmer, brighter tones. We added some burnt orange and red in the cushions and the painting, and it lifted the whole room, and gave it a homeness it might otherwise have lacked."

LIGHTING *In addition to more unobtrusive mono-point lights and downlights, there are table lamps by Christian Liaigre and these sculptural hanging lamps, which have a strong, almost Art Deco shape and emit a calm, uniform light.*

ELECTRONICS *The custommade cabinets have been designed to house, and to hide when necessary, the television, stereo, and video machines. The beauty of specially made accommodation is that wiring is also made invisible.*

TEXTILES *Fabrics are predominantly plain, so differences in texture are more noticeable. Linen scrim, with its rough, loose weave, makes the ideal contemporary net curtain. Other fabrics used include velour and fake ostrich leather.*

FURNITURE *Chairs, sofa, and coffee table are all by Christian Liaigre. The clients already owned the dining table and chairs. Since they are similar in color to the floor, David Mullman "lifted" them on a rectangle of coir matting bound with a dark linen border.*

COLOR *The clients wanted an uncompromisingly modern look and were wedded to a palette of neutrals, grounded by the glossy chocolate of the floor. David Mullman persuaded them that warmer accents would prevent the apartment from feeling too cold.*

FLOORING *The windows and oak floor are original. The floor has been stained very dark brown and polished to a high sheen. Its rich glow provides character and the warmth of a natural material, as well as grounding the color scheme of the whole apartment.*

THE SCALE OF THE CEILING FIXTURES GIVES THEM A STRONG SCULPTURAL PRESENCE IN THIS PERFECTLY POISED INTERIOR.

Crucial to the success of these lean, clean interiors is somewhere to hide the mess of family life. David Mullman created a custommade storage unit for the living room in dark, textured oak, which matches the floor. Sliding screens of frosted glass, framed in bronze, pull across to hide the television and the stereo, and there are cupboards beneath for books, CDs, videos, and magazines. A further wall of built-in cupboards in the dining room is similarly packed.

When line and color are as disciplined as this, texture plays an important role. Fabrics are a mix of heavy linens and cottons. Two layers of linen scrim screen out the view of the building opposite, but allow plenty of light to wash in through the trio of high windows. The Christian Liaigre easy chair is covered in fake ostrich leather, which the owners like because it reminds them of their native Australia.

In addition to the table and floor lamps, also by Christian Liaigre, and the recessed lights, which pick out the cabinet and the Garnier vase in the window alcove, there are large hanging ceiling fixtures. Their scale, as much as their shape, gives them a strong sculptural presence in this perfectly poised interior.

RIGHT **Right angles dominate this view of the living room. Three black and white photographs of the clients' little girl make a graphic display framed in matching black. The frosted-glass sliding doors of the made-to-measure cabinet are framed in bronze. Capacious cupboards beneath hide all the unsightly detritus of family life, allowing the room to retain its uncluttered dignity. Even books are lined up perfectly.**

ABOVE **The layout of the apartment with its internal hall dictated that the dining room has no window. Instead it borrows some of the ample light that floods into the huge living room windows. In addition to the wide doorway between the two rooms, David Mullman carved out a large internal window, to line up exactly with the dining table. In fact, the dining room is more often used in the evenings, when natural light is not an issue.**

KITCHENS

In an age when gadgets and machinery do much of the work once left to cooks and scullery maids, and when making a meal is marketed as a leisure activity to be celebrated in glossy books and glamorous television programs, the kitchen has a new place at the center of the modern home. No longer just a factory for food production, the contemporary kitchen may also be a room for relaxing, for getting together with friends and family, for cooking and eating as a pleasurable, communal activity. So, it isn't enough for today's kitchen to be efficient and ergonomically sound; it must also be stylish and comfortable. The modern kitchen has to fulfill so many functions that its design demands particularly careful thought. Whether large enough to accommodate a sofa and a couple of armchairs or pocket-sized, whether open-plan or self-contained, the kitchens on the following pages provide a fund of clever ideas, both practical and inspirational.

THE HEIGHT OF GRANDEUR In the eighteenth century, this kitchen was a reception room. Its high ceiling and lofty sash windows demanded a modern and practical design that could live up to the elegance of the past.

The grander the house, the more difficult it can be to adapt it for modern life. The original kitchens of this splendid Georgian townhouse in Salisbury's Cathedral Close were in the basement. Fortunately perhaps for the current owners, a previous occupant had decided to take the plunge and convert a former living room on the raised ground floor into a kitchen. The decorative plasterwork of its soaring ceiling remains as evidence of its original status.

The change of use makes sense. After all, the contemporary kitchen has risen up the social ladder to become a reception room in its own right. No longer the hidden haunt of flushed cooks and sweaty scullery maids, the kitchen is where we welcome friends and choose to dine. There is, however, a potential clash of aesthetics when it comes to fitting the storage space and appliances that we require for a kitchen to be functional into a space designed for gilt-framed oil paintings and elegant sofas.

When interior designer Helen Ellery was hired to redecorate, she knew at once that the old kitchen had to go. "It was messy, and dark, and not very functional," she remembers. "I wanted something that was much more light and streamlined, and I wanted the style to be traditional without being twee or 'period,' and with a modern twist."

In collaboration with kitchen designers Plain English, Helen devised a scheme that is beautifully simple, entirely practical, and perfectly in keeping with the architectural bones of the room. Cupboards

in painted wood wrap around three walls. Their detailing is minimal; a shallow fielded panel with no additional moldings, and modest handles. Opposite the two tall sash windows with their shutters and deep window seats, she set a generous double ceramic sink. Above it is a huge plate rack, shelving for pots and pans and a stainless-steel rod for hanging utensils. Cupboards on each side are arranged symmetrically.

On the fireplace wall, the chimney breast encloses the stove and, above it, a powerful extractor fan. An oversized clock above the mantelshelf reinforces this as the focus of the room, just as it would always have been. To the right of the chimney breast there is a specially made built-in hutch with glass doors. "I like glass doors on kitchen cupboards. I like to see what is inside and also they break up the heaviness of rows of solid doors," she explains.

The symmetry and large-scale simplicity of the design echo the Georgian proportions of the room. The high ceilings, however, remained a problem. Ellery's clever solution was to install a deep plate shelf on brackets at a level that fits more comfortably with the height of the kitchen cupboards. It brings the eye down and make the room feel less cavernous.

For the modern twists, Helen chose a sharp, almost acidic yellow in crunchy linen to make Roman shades for the windows and to cover the window seat cushions. Together with the glint and gleam of shiny metal and brushed stainless steel, the color adds contemporary spice to this venerable interior.

Big rooms need bold decorative gestures. The design of the kitchen cupboards is extremely plain, if traditional, and is given weight by the hefty moldings and chunky shelving. The plate shelf on brackets, which successfully lowers the height of the ceiling to a level more appropriate for an informal room, is also chunky, and mirrors the mantelpiece (BELOW LEFT). The only small element of the design is the cupboard handles. Big wooden knobs tend to give a kitchen a Toytown tweeness. Glass doors break up the visual monotony of the wall cupboards, which are arranged symmetrically facing the windows. The central plate rack, shelves, and hooks for utensils, make accessible storage for well-used items, conveniently close to the dishwasher, which is disguised behind a cupboard door next to the sink.

ABOVE Glass doors allow a view into the brilliant white space of a room that has content as well as style. The cupboards and work surfaces are white laminate with aluminum trim. Walls are bright white, and appliances, china, and utensils white or stainless steel (ABOVE RIGHT). The room is saved from operating-room sterility by the rich patina of the wooden floor and other warming and softening elements such as the wooden Venetian blinds and the leather-covered chairs. Instead the effect is of pure efficiency. The peninsular work surface incorporates the burners so the sociable cook can continue a conversation with guests. The well-trodden triangle between stove, sink, and fridge has been observed, with the fridge on the wall opposite the sink, and the right kind of storage is provided in the right places.

PURELY PRACTICAL

Clean, contemporary, and spotless, this whiter-than-white kitchen in a chic London flat was designed to be as much of a pleasure to cook in as to look at.

When designer Rob Gelling of Bulthaup was called in to create a kitchen for this luxurious bachelor apartment, he knew the look should be clean and contemporary, and that the client enjoyed cooking for friends. "The rest of the apartment is modern and simple, but uses very high quality materials," he explains. "I didn't think the style of the kitchen should compete with that richness and, as there was already a beautiful wooden floor, I felt I could use pure white without the risk of it looking too sterile or clinical."

The snowy white laminate, which clothes the kitchen units and work surfaces, is contrasted with an aluminum trim. "I chose anodized aluminum rather than stainless steel," he says, "because the effect is softer and more domestic." Glass doors lead into the kitchen, and there are two large windows. There

is also a transparent glass and Plexiglas table. Walls are painted white, and all the china, utensils, and tableware are either white or shiny metal. As a result, the room is incredibly bright; light pours in from all directions through the windows and the glass doors, and is reflected back in abundance.

Pristine good looks aside, the kitchen is also extremely practical. Its layout is designed for the sociable cook, with the burners mounted on a peninsula, at right angles to the sink. "This area between sink and stove is the most heavily used of any kitchen, the place where you stand most often when cooking," says Rob. "By turning the stove to face outwards, you can cook while continuing a conversation with friends sitting at the table." And, just to add to the sociability, there is space for someone to stand on the other side to chop an onion or stir a sauce.

Opposite the sink is a row of tall units, which include the raised double oven and a huge stainless-steel fridge. These have been placed so they can be reached without the need to push past the person who is cooking. In kitchen design jargon, this is called "getting the flows right" and, as anyone who has tried helping out in a badly designed

kitchen will know, it is just as important as the provision of enough storage space.

Putting the right things in the right places is second nature to the experienced kitchen designer. And so we have pots and pans, and oils and spices near the stove; a trash can in a drawer, which pulls out from under the sink; and deep china drawers next to the dishwasher. There is also an area of dedicated work surface where appliances such as the toaster, coffee maker, and food processor can be left plugged in, and hidden away behind a sliding shutter when not in use. Above are little drawers for teabags, medicines, and all those other fiddly kitchen bits that get shoved to the back of bigger drawers and lost. If extra work surface is required, there is a trolley that can be wheeled into play.

All in all, this is a kitchen that combines form and function flawlessly. Even the handles have been carefully considered. Elegant rods of aluminum, they are easy to grab and set far enough above the cupboard and drawer fronts that the laminate won't be scratched by a ring, or stained by oily fingers.

THE ROOM IS INCREDIBLY BRIGHT; LIGHT POURS IN THROUGH THE WINDOWS AND THE GLASS DOORS, AND IS REFLECTED BACK IN ABUNDANCE.

ABOVE **The bachelor owner of this ultimate bachelor pad enjoys cooking and entertaining—whether dinner for two at the glass and Plexiglas kitchen table, or for more seated at the dining table. Rattan place** mats soften the clank of china and flatware on glass, but the color scheme of white, silver, and black is continued.
RIGHT **Pans, colanders, and strainers are stored on open shelves for easy access.**

ABOVE **Opposite the stove is a coffee-making area. To its right there is another work surface where a kettle, toaster, and food processor can be left plugged in. They are hidden when not in use behind a metal roller shutter.**

RIGHT **The wall opposite the sink holds a range of tall cupboards, a double oven, and a huge fridge. The trolley acts as an extra work surface and can be wheeled into play when required. Above it is a wall-mounted television for those evenings spent cooking for one.**

LEFT AND RIGHT **This garden room fills the space that was once an outdoor terrace and which, according to Angela, was "dank and redundant." Thanks to French doors and a generous ceiling lantern, the room is quite the opposite, warmed by the sun in the morning, even in winter, and opening straight into the garden in summer when the doors are left open.**

THE FAMILY KITCHEN Angela A'Court's kitchen has space and light in spades, thanks to a radical remodeling of the ground floor of her Victorian row house and the sacrifice of a dark, damp terrace.

Artist Angela A'Court remodeled the ground floor of her Victorian row house. She lost a dining room, a breakfast room, and an outdoor terrace, but she gained a huge L-shaped combined kitchen, dining, and living room. "We found we never used a separate dining room," she explains. "We don't tend to entertain formally, so it was wasted space. And the terrace was dark and dank because it didn't get enough sun."

The terrace was enclosed to make an extra room and given a large, circular skylight and a wall of French doors, so it has the bright, light atmosphere of a conservatory. A wide opening was created in the wall of the former breakfast room so that this new garden room leads straight off the kitchen, and the wall that divided the kitchen from the breakfast room was also knocked down. The ex-dining room is now a playroom which, in turn, leads into the garden room. There is still a living room at the front of the house. The back of the house faces east so the family find they use the garden room in the mornings and can follow the sun as it sets and light floods into the rooms at the front.

Being able to follow the sun is only one of many advantages of this new layout. In the modern

FAR RIGHT **The built-in hutch is original and a reminder of the days when the ground floor was divided into smaller rooms, including a kitchen and a scullery. It is painted dark French gray, against which Angela's collection of sunny contemporary pottery, including pieces by Lizzie Hodges, stands out in bright contrast. The modern pots enliven the old carpentry, and the Habitat table and chairs sit next to it equally happily. In a color scheme of warm neutrals, sludgy greens, mustard yellows, and dusty blues, the tomato reds of the picture frames add a dash of spice.**

LEFT Rather than consign the old kitchen cupboards to a dumpster, Angela took the more creative and less wasteful route and adapted them to suit the style of her new kitchen. The cupboards, with paneling copied from the Victorian built-in hutch, once had chunky Arts and Crafts-style handles. Angela swapped these for small, square handles with a more contemporary feel and added the row of low wall cupboards and the chunky shelving with its line-up of old metal storage jars.

THIS PICTURE **A modern sofa in the garden room is slightly recessed in an alcove, which adds depth and architectural interest to an otherwise blank wall. Inside the alcove Angela has painted a very simple, monochrome mural featuring her favourite birds, crows. The painting has the fresh, free style of a fresco and contributes to the outdoor, slightly Mediterranean feel of the room, as do the plants. A pair of matching side tables gives the arrangement a strong symmetry.**

household where cooking and eating are communal activities and where socializing tends to center on the kitchen table, the "living" kitchen, which combines the spaces where you prepare and eat food and still leaves room enough for a sofa and comfortable armchair or two, has become a domestic ideal. Instead of being closeted in a basement or cramped little back room, the person doing the cooking can still keep an eye on the children or have a conversation with guests. The kitchen table becomes a focus of family life, whether for eating together, for playing games and making things, or for doing homework.

Angela wanted her newly extended kitchen to fulfill all these functions; to be light, bright, and modern in feel, and to be practical. Thanks to

the French doors and the skylight, the room is always bright. Further light is reflected from the cream walls and the pale limestone flooring, which has been laid throughout. Furnishings, like the plain kitchen table, the natural wood shelving and wall cupboards, and huge antique pine linen press, conform to the same palette. The darkest color in the scheme is reserved for the original built-in hutch and kitchen cupboards, which were made to match it. These are painted a subtle shade of French gray. Angela's collection of contemporary pottery, grouped on the hutch, stands out in bold splashes of yellow, blue, and terra-cotta against this strong but neutral color.

Rather than replace the carpentry in the kitchen to match her brand new open-plan room, Angela chose to update it. The large Arts and Crafts-style

INSTEAD OF PICTURES ON THE WALL, THERE IS A MURAL PAINTED BY ANGELA, A STRIP OF CHALKY COLOR ENCLOSING FOUR SILHOUETTED CROWS.

ARCHITECTURE *By extending the opening in the original chimney breast up toward the ceiling, Angela created an alcove for the kitchen table and space for shelves above, where everyday dishes are conveniently stored ready for meal times.*

PICTURES *There are only a handful of pictures hanging in these rooms. In all cases, they are quite small and are placed, as here, on appropriately small areas of wall so they are framed architecturally, rather than looking lost in the middle of nowhere.*

WALLS *Walls throughout are painted pale cream with a tinge of green. This is quite a warm neutral and complements the pale sand of the stone floor. The simple frescolike painting above the sofa seems appropriate in a room that bridges the indoors and garden.*

FLOORING *Large square tiles of pale limestone flow through the room from the kitchen and dining area to the informal seating area. A stone floor adds architectural gravity to any room and has the added advantage that underfloor heating can be installed.*

PATTERN *Small areas of pattern have a big impact in a room where plain surfaces dominate. This large-scale floral design adds an air of old-fashioned comfort. The baggy slipcover is informal in keeping with this relaxed room.*

TEXTILES *A sofa and armchairs in a kitchen are an invitation to linger. The clean lines of the contemporary sofa are softened by the throw and extra-large pillows, while the capacious armchairs with matching stools are a more traditional design.*

metal handles on cupboards and drawers were replaced by smaller, square metal handles for a more urban and sophisticated look. New chunky wood shelving was put above the sink, and a line of slim wall cupboards with distinctly contemporary proportions was added. Although relatively small, these stylistic changes have transformed the character of the woodwork from period charm to crisp modernity.

The strictly contemporary feel continues into the garden room, which is sparsely, if comfortably furnished with a modern sofa flanked by modern chests and a pair of capacious armchairs with matching footstools. Instead of pictures on the wall, there is a mural painted by Angela, a strip of chalky color enclosing four silhouetted crows. The effect is frescolike and combines with the potted plants and view of sky and clouds to make the room feel like a bridge between indoors and

outdoors, even in winter when the French doors are kept firmly closed.

Aside from the aesthetics of this elegantly informal space, there are many practical touches. The table slots neatly into the alcove where there was once a fireplace. By extending this alcove to the same height as the built-in hutch, Angela created space for more shelving. "I wanted everything to be accessible," she explains, "so that is where we keep the dishes that we use every day." Next to the table is a whole wall of blackboard. "It's the most brilliant aide-memoire," says Angela, who scribbles notes for herself daily, making sure to put them near the top of the board where the children can't reach to erase them.

ABOVE **Just behind the alcove where the kitchen table sits was the wall that separated the kitchen from the breakfast room. The floor-to-ceiling blackboard beyond it is the perfect place for scribbling all those things you might otherwise forget. The antique linen press is both handsome and functional, providing ample storage space and the drama of a single, very large piece of furniture.**

RIGHT AND ABOVE LEFT
Different textures make the sofa look extra welcoming. The upholstery is taupe bouclé weave wool (2), with cushions in bouclé and lemon-green chenille (1). Further texture is provided by the loose-weave linen mix of the Roman shades (4). The Designers Guild floral linen (3), which covers the armchairs, brings all the other colors together.

ANTIQUE CHIC The kitchen of Milan antique dealer Maurizio Epifani is furnished with pieces that would look equally at home in his shop. Even the flatware and pans have the patina of age, proving that practicality is not just the preserve of the new.

ABOVE The room is full of beautiful things to look at, like this display of eighteenth-century French pottery plates hanging above the table. Versions of the same pottery with its plain creamy glaze and distinctive curvy edges are still made in France, and these Maurizio uses as everyday china. The old knives and forks with their well-worn wooden handles would be wasted hidden in a drawer, so they are stacked in a basket ready for use.

RIGHT Maurizio designed the cupboards and open shelves, taking his cue from antique originals, and had them made by a craftsman. The asymmetrical layout of cubby holes and little cupboards is unusual and made more so by the selection of quirky handles, which include a branch of orange coral, sparkly crystal, and bronze animal heads. Frequently used mugs and utensils hang on hooks above the double sink and stove, while knives and wooden spoons are stored in a pot by the draining board.

THE APARTMENT IS FURNISHED WITH A MIX OF PRECIOUS, AND SOMETIMES PECULIAR, PIECES FROM ALL OVER THE WORLD.

The website for Maurizio Epifani's Milan antiques shop opens with a Jack Russell terrier appearing like the Metro-Goldwyn-Mayer lion, through a loop of golden riband. The eccentricities continue with a small animated dog showing the way to the store by trotting rather jerkily along the lines of a street map, a reptile that spits out a series of animal sculptures, and a flying Botticelli Venus.

Maurizio's shop is a rich source of the unusual, the amusing, the decorative, and the rare, "from ancient Egypt to Coca-Cola," as he likes to say. It is hardly surprising then, that his apartment in Milan is furnished with a mix of precious, and sometimes peculiar, pieces from all over the world and from many different centuries. Even his kitchen, which is small, is packed with visual interest.

This long, fairly narrow room has the advantage of a single tall window, which opens onto a balcony, so although space is limited, there is always light in abundance. In his choice of decoration and layout Maurizio has made the most of a space that could easily have felt cramped. Crisp ceramic floor tiles are laid diagonally in a black and white checkerboard, creating an optical effect that appears to widen the space. Cupboards, shelves, drawers, the double sink, and all appliances are ranged along one wall only, leaving the other wall free for a table and two chairs.

Aside from the built-in cupboards, which Maurizio had made to his own design, the table and chairs are the only furnishings. But, instead of the usual stripped pine and plywood, his table and chairs are fine, if sturdy and eminently usable, antiques. The table is walnut and incorporates a flatware drawer, and the chairs are eighteenth-century French and extremely comfortable. There is a dining room in the apartment, but the kitchen is where most meals are enjoyed, either alone or with a couple of friends.

The colors in this room are muted and sophisticated. The walls are off-white, as are the cupboards and all other woodwork. A low molding around the walls helps to bring the ceiling height down. The walls above this molding are painted the color of sand. There are no pictures on the walls, but instead there is a display of eighteenth-century French earthenware plates above the table. Their

THIS PAGE The table and pair of chairs are elegant furnishings in their own right, but low-key enough not to look out of place in a kitchen. The table is Italian and made of walnut and the chairs are eighteenth-century French, in a design that is still widely copied today as it is comfortable and pretty. Their rubbed paintwork picks up the shade of sand Maurizio used above the picture rail. The tall, skinny antique lamp casts a good, localized downlight for dining, but the antique terra-cotta chicken is only a temporary resident at the table, making way for plates and napkins when a friend comes to dine.

OPPOSITE Close-ups of some of the details that make this kitchen such an interesting place to sit and eat. The carved marble draining board (BELOW LEFT) is a typically Italian feature.

colors are plain and faded, warm creams and well-washed grays, but their glossy, uneven texture and the restrained curves of their decorated rims make a pleasingly subtle display. Maurizio uses plates like these, which are still made in France, every day, and there is often a pile of them stacked to dry on his marble draining board.

This is a kitchen where things that are used often have the patina and appeal of the antique. The flatware, for example, which is stored in a basket, has smooth wooden handles—not the sort of knives and forks you can throw in the dishwasher, but a pleasure to eat with. Even the pans and the strainer that hang above the sink have the worn and polished look of utensils with a long history, and almost every handle on the drawers and cupboards is different and antique—one is coral, two are crystal, others are bronze. While the most important consideration when designing a kitchen should be practicality, Maurizio Epifani's kitchen is an example of how practicality need not exclude beauty and individuality.

LEFT **There are not many kitchen sinks you could describe as enchanting, but this must be the exception. The combination of "Nordic White" paintwork on the match-boarding and window frames, bright white enamel, the transparent linen shades, the old-fashioned white china lamp and tureens, and the scattering of terra-cotta pots frilled with flowers in white and palest pink adds up to a setting for washing dishes that is as pretty as a picture. The view is pretty, too; a white wall topped by geraniums.**

SIMPLY SWEDISH The Swedish artist Carl Larsson, whose paintings of cottage interiors were so influential at the turn of the last century, called one of his books *Lasst Licht Hinein* (Let in the Light). He would approve of this kitchen.

Swedish designer and shop owner Moussie Sayers is teased by her family for her favorite piece of decorating advice: "Bring in the light." "I say it so often," she laughs, "that is has become a kind of mantra." Her London shop, Nordic Style, sells furniture, accessories, fabrics, and paints inspired by the late-eighteenth-century Gustavian interiors of her home country. Colors are typically pale and fresh, blinds are translucent, china is plain white. In short, everything is designed in accordance with her mantra.

Moussie Sayers' London home is a showcase for the things she sells in her shop and an inspiration for anyone wishing to import classical Swedish elegance and "bring in the light" to their own house. The lower ground floor kitchen of her semi-detached late Victorian house was already blessed with a row of two arched windows and a partially glazed arched doorway. But the way she has decorated makes the most of this natural light and imparts a clean airiness to the room that is refreshingly bright, even in the depths of winter.

The character of the room relies on painted wood. The walls are lined with match-boarding, the simplest and least expensive form of paneling, which is painted soft white and also backs the wooden kitchen counters and covers the wall between the windows behind the glistening white enamel sink. The floor and wall cupboards with their typically Swedish diamond motif (copied from eighteenth-century Gustavian furnishings) are also painted white, but with an overglaze of antique white, which gives the color more depth and texture and makes the cupboards look as though they have always been there. The graceful wooden chairs, copies of eighteenth-century originals, are white, as is the base of the English pine table. Even the wooden floorboards have been painted, in a bleached checkerboard of cream and sage.

Other typically Swedish touches are the potted geraniums on the windowsill, which glow a brilliant green as the sunlight filters through their leaves, and the adjustable lamps with their white china shades, which hang over the table and the sink. "We call

THIS PAGE **The pots on the windowsill are, according to Moussie Sayers, a very Swedish touch and are reminiscent of Larsson's paintings of his own cottage interiors. In a room where colors are creamy and muted, the jewel green leaves seem to glow more brightly in the sunshine.**
LEFT **The kitchen cupboards were hand built. They are painted the same Nordic White as the walls and match-boarding (1), but have been subtly dragged with an Antique White glaze (3), giving them an instant patina of age.**

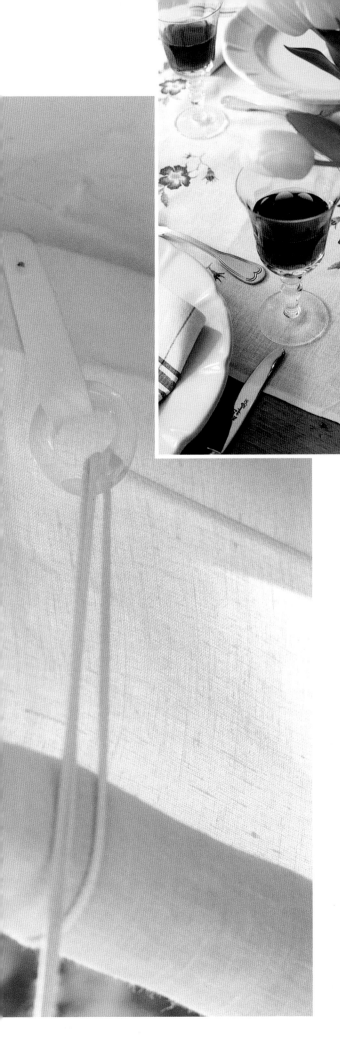

FAR LEFT AND ABOVE
The antique table with its
scrubbed pine top is laid
with pieces from Nordic
Style, mixing the elaborate
with the plain for an effect
that is elegantly informal.
Most elaborate are the
metal candlesticks, which
are direct copies of an
eighteenth-century design.
The glasses and flatware
are taken from plainer
eighteenth-century originals,
but the pure linen table
runner with its scattering of
red dog roses is Moussie's
own design (2, previous
page), part of a line of
fabrics including checks and
stripes in complementary
colors. Around the table are
Leksand chairs, another
Sayers interpretation of a
Gustavian classic.
LEFT The unlined shades let
in plenty of light even when
partially lowered and have a
softer silhouette than Roman
or roller shades, thanks to
the way they unfurl.
ABOVE RIGHT An
adjustable "cobbler's lamp"
above the dining table can
be lowered for an intimate
evening atmosphere.

these 'cobbler's lamps' in Sweden," Moussie says.
"They cast a diffused pool of light for a more
relaxed and intimate atmosphere when the ceiling
spotlights are not required. Although, of course, for
dinner, we always have candles."

The appeal of this gentle, romantic style is that it is
classical without being either grand or obviously
old-fashioned. Its historical inspiration dates back to
the eighteenth-century home interiors, which were
in turn inspired by the Swedish King Gustav's visit to
the French court. French interior design at the time
represented the very acme of refined taste. Distilled
and much simplified for the homes of the middle
classes, the Swedish interpretation retained the
elegance of French courtly style, but shed its
excesses. What has come to be known as "Gustavian"
style appeals to modern tastes for its restraint and
lack of frills and fussiness.

Moussie Sayers' kitchen is an example of how
readily the Gustavian look can be adopted in a
modern home, and how easy it is to live with.
Glass, china, and even the candlesticks are
reproductions, and they are also eminently usable.
Only the table linen, which is from Moussie's own
line of fabrics, uses an entirely new design—a simple
scattering of dog roses on a plain, white linen
runner. But the spirit of the design—pretty without
being twee, elegant without being formal—is true
to Gustavian precedent.

The Italians are never afraid of bumping high-tech straight up against the old-fashioned, the traditional, or the handmade. In this room all three collide with considerable panache, as the uneven terra-cotta floor tiles meet the flawless stainless-steel kick-boards, and the clean right angles of the modern cupboards face the twisty metal legs of the antique table.

CULTURE CLASH

From one end, this Milanese kitchen has a fiercely industrial look, from the other a relaxed, almost country feel. Mix the two for Italian style and efficiency.

When Italian interior designer Daniela Micol Wajskol accepted a commission to work on this early-twentieth-century apartment in Milan, she took on much more than its decoration. The internal layout was radically changed and a whole new floor gained by building up into the roof. The glamorous kitchen was originally two rooms, but is now big enough for informal dining as well as housing an impressive battery of high-tech equipment.

The design of this room is a fine example of how period elegance, rustic charm, and uncompromising modernity can be brought together in a genuinely harmonious blend of old and new. The room has the graceful proportions of a reception room, with a high ceiling and two tall casement windows with

paneled recesses. A less adventurous designer might have plumped for a traditional kitchen, perhaps with cupboards paneled to match the old woodwork.

Daniela's clients are enthusiastic cooks and wanted to enjoy all the advantages that contemporary kitchen technology has to offer. Daniela chose a kitchen by Arc Linea, an Italian company, in silky stainless steel and pale beech. Storage provided by the stainless-steel-fronted drawers and beech cupboards is supplemented by custommade carpentry with shelves the right size for storing bottles and magazines.

At the working end of the kitchen, everything is designed for maximum efficiency and practicality. There are, for example, three sinks, two set into the work surface beneath the window, and one for food preparation, set into the stainless-steel work surface of the island unit. This unit, with its drawers and cupboards beneath, also holds a commercial meat slicer for the whole hams and salamis the owners buy when visiting the countryside.

The oven, which is a gleaming expanse of stainless steel, has a similarly industrial look, as if it were straight from the kitchens of a grand restaurant.

ABOVE LEFT **At the working end of the kitchen all is geared toward steely efficiency. The owners of the apartment enjoy cooking for themselves and for friends, and the appliances are designed to make catering for large numbers as easy as possible. There are even two extractor fans above the extended stovetop to spirit away double the steam and odor. At the other end of the room (ABOVE RIGHT), all is sweetness and light with pretty folding chairs, flowers, and checked shades at the casement windows.**

ARCHITECTURE *The apartment was completely reorganized internally and extra rooms gained by building into the roof space. These extra rooms gave the owners the flexibility to lose a room by knocking two into one to make a large kitchen.*

APPLIANCES *The kitchen units are beech and stainless steel, and the appliances are stainless steel to match. All have been chosen for maximum capacity, giving the kitchen a professional feel. There are three sinks, one specifically for washing and preparing food.*

WALLS *Flat cream latex has been used on the walls, and the woodwork is painted the same shade in eggshell. This background uniformity makes the room look larger and provides a plain and undemanding foil for the drama of shiny metal and pale wood.*

FLOORING *Daniela chose a traditional Italian terra-cotta tile for the floor, made from local clay. The color is a gentle apricot, and the matt texture is slightly uneven, giving a handmade quality. Large squares, laid diagonally, make the room look larger.*

FURNITURE *The folding chairs and antique table are light pieces that can be put aside when floor space is required for entertaining. Although the traditional style of the chairs is in sharp contrast with the kitchen units, the pale beech is a perfect match.*

STORAGE *Custommade storage was added in the triangle of space under the stairs to supplement the kitchen cupboards. Shelves and cubby holes designed specially to hold ranks of bottles and jars, and even magazines, turn everyday items into an attractive display.*

LEFT **Despite the wholesale remodeling of the apartment, which dates from the early 1900s, none of its period charm has been lost. Casement windows still have their original brass handles, and the delicate moldings of the paneling that surrounds them have also been preserved. The unlined checked linen shades look as good with the pretty orchid in its woven basket as they do at the working end of the kitchen surrounded by slick stainless steel.**

THIS ROOM IS A FINE EXAMPLE OF HOW PERIOD ELEGANCE, RUSTIC CHARM, AND MODERNITY CAN BE BROUGHT TOGETHER.

There is an additional gas burner designed for cooking fish at the side of its six burners. And hanging above there are two extractor fans for double the power. Needless to say, the fridge is also huge and incorporates an ice and water dispenser for those hot Milanese summers. Built around and totally encasing the fridge are further cupboards for food storage.

There is no doubt that a kitchen of this scale and modernity is an extremely effective work station. The disadvantage is that your kitchen can end up looking like somewhere to work rather than enjoy yourself. Daniela has softened the industrial feel by introducing old-fashioned materials and a very slightly battered antique table with twisted metal legs.

For the floor she chose large Italian "cotta" tiles made from baked terra-cotta. Their pale, gentle color and handmade feel make an interesting contrast where they meet with the slick metal kick-boards of the kitchen units. Other softening touches are provided by the slim Roman shades in an unlined linen check and the flowers that always sit on the table and the windowsills. The folding cane and beech chairs with tie-on cushions are not old, but they are traditional.

As in all rooms that successfully mix styles and periods, the visual pleasure of this kitchen comes from its surprising juxtapositions, as if the eye is forced to appreciate something afresh because it is unexpected.

ABOVE **The chairs and table have an outdoors, old-fashioned café feel, perfect for a breakfast cup of coffee. Colors and textures—the rubbed planks of the table, the bleached terra-cotta of the floor, and the soft gray of the cushions—are gentle and muted, and materials are natural and earthy—clay, wood, cane, and linen, all in marked contrast with the other end of the room, where the serious business of cooking takes place.**
LEFT **Even a humble bottle of soda looks as smart as a soldier when lined up in perfect formation.**

HALLS

A hall is not an essential. Many open-plan interiors are designed without one, and in houses and apartments of more conventional layout, the hall often seems the room most easily sacrificed in the drive to knock down internal walls and to open out space. But a hall is more than just an entrance, it is also a very useful room. Often it encloses the stairs and helps to insulate other rooms from the noise of traffic between floors. It is a neutral space into which you can invite strangers. It provides a transition between outdoors and indoors, somewhere to prop wet umbrellas, dump bags of shopping, leave muddy boots, and hang up coats and hats. A big hall is space well wasted. Like that other spatial indulgence, a large landing, it gives a house an air of relaxed grandeur. But even a small hall, carefully designed, can provide a visual welcome, as well as invaluable space for hanging, propping, and dumping things.

THIS PICTURE **A wide** strip of Wilton carpet runs up the middle of the stairs to meet a wall-to-wall Wilton in a coordinated stripe on the landing. Stairs and banisters have been painted in two different shades of neutral, both from Farrow & Ball. This gives a more streamlined effect than the usual treatment of old stairs, which tends to leave treads and banister rails as bare wood in contrast with painted banisters and baseboards.

LEFT **A large landing makes a house feel spacious and can also be commandeered as an extra, open-plan room. Children like to play on a big landing because it feels like space at the very center of a house, not cloistered in a far corner. This landing is a grown-up space for playing, kitted out with everything you need to relax with a good book— a comfortable sofa with plenty of big cushions** (RIGHT AND BELOW), **somewhere to put your cup of coffee or glass of wine, and excellent light, thanks to the generous sash window.**

MAKING A LANDING Fay Morgan and
Roger Oates have optimized limited space in the long, narrow hall of their Georgian country house, and created a whole new room on their second-floor landing.

Roger Oates and Fay Morgan's house has a front door that opens onto the street. The ground on which the house is built slopes quite steeply down toward the back, so the door at that end of the hall opens well above ground level. Instead of steps leading straight down from the back door, Roger and Fay have built a spacious platform with wooden stairs.

"In fact, we have effectively turned the house back to front," explains Fay. "We never use the front door, so the back door has become the main entrance." This new arrangement works particularly well in the summer. The kitchen leads off the hall at the back of the house, and they often carry breakfast out to the table and chairs on their spacious back-door balcony.

The hall is long, but not particularly wide, like so many halls in houses of this size and period. To relieve the effect of a long, thin corridor, they have used different wall colors and flooring to divide it into two distinct spaces. The far end of the hall, where it narrows beyond the staircase, is painted a warm and welcoming red, while the floor is covered in wall-to-wall coconut matting. This is an extremely practical, cheap, and surprisingly good-looking way to carpet a small entrance hall, and helps to get shoes dry and well brushed by the time feet reach the stairs.

THE FAR END OF THE HALL, WHERE IT NARROWS BEYOND THE STAIRCASE, IS PAINTED A WARM AND WELCOMING RED.

RIGHT The entrance to the house has been turned back to front. The main entrance is now through the back door, which is above ground level because of the way the land slopes. The back door opens onto a spacious wooden platform, big enough for breakfast on summer mornings, and a flight of wooden steps. The

hall is divided into two distinct zones by color and flooring. The far end has wall-to-wall coconut matting, more often seen cut into small oblongs to make doormats, and walls painted a rich, welcoming red (4, opposite). The staircase hall is Farrow & Ball's Off White, its original floorboards

quietened by a runner in a brown and cream herringbone weave (2), which picks up the colors of the stair carpet (3). ABOVE Rolled rugs such as these and (1) are the current occupants of a capacious basket at the far end of the hall, which, like the stool by the stairs, is useful "dumping space."

At the staircase end of the hall, walls are off-white to maximize light, and the original floorboards are stained dark mahogany. The flatweave runner is kept in place by an antislip rubberized mesh, which prevents it from moving around and wrinkling on the smooth wood.

In order to keep the effect as plain as possible in this relatively small space, the banisters and banister rail are painted the same off-white as other woodwork, while the stairs themselves and their baseboards are a slightly darker shade of stone. Running up the middle of the stairs is a Roger Oates striped Wilton carpet. The pile and underlay mean that even the heaviest tread is muffled. Stair carpet gets particularly heavy wear, and underlay also helps to prolong its life. If you are particularly assiduous, as Fay points out, you can shunt a stair runner up or down a few inches to spread the wear more evenly. The generous landing is also carpeted, in a finer stripe, designed to coordinate with the stair carpet.

Because the front door is never used, this is the end of the hall where coats are hung on hooks on each side of the door. If this were the main entrance, their bulk might feel constricting as you came through the door. The only other furnishings are a basket for newspapers or anything else that needs a temporary home, and a stool for putting things on, or sitting on to put on or take off shoes.

The landing has become a room in its own right, thanks to the lure of the comfortable linen-draped sofa and pile of books. "It's a particularly nice place to read," comments Fay. "It faces west, and the light is lovely." A leather trunk serves as a coffee table and somewhere to put your feet up.

COOL RECEPTION Grand archways bestow space and light on the hall of a smart Milanese apartment, where the decoration is restrained and sophisticated, but the welcome is warm.

Despite appearances, the elegant hall of this apartment in Milan is entirely new. The staircase is new, the paneling is new, and the floor is new. The space is the result of knocking two apartments into one, but neither had a staircase as neither had a second floor. The upstairs, with its leafy roof terrace, was once uninhabited and inaccessible attic storage. Designer Daniela Micol Wajskol, who was originally commissioned to roll the two apartments into one, immediately saw the potential for further expansion into the roof, and eventually managed to persuade the Milanese planning authorities that she was right.

The apartment is part of a much larger building. The hall is on an inner wall and has to rely on borrowed light. This lack of hall windows is typical of layouts in houses as well as apartments, hence the popularity of the front door fanlight or stained glass panel and, in grander houses, the staircase lantern, which allows light to pour in through the roof. Daniela has made sure that this hall gains light from two directions. At the top of the staircase she installed a whole wall of windows and a French door leading onto the roof terrace. Light from this window spills down the stairs. The hall also gains borrowed light from the right, through the tall windows of the living room and dining room, which open out from it through wide archways. More daylight is reflected at the foot of the stairs by the console mirror.

The archways are a clever means of making all three rooms appear more spacious. The hallway enjoys views through two large reception rooms, which both benefit from the whole width of the apartment. Paneling to dado level unites the spaces architecturally, as does the oak-planked floor. There is also a doorway between the reception rooms, so this whole area is almost, but not quite, open-plan.

Although the effect of opening out these rooms is similar in terms of light and the flow of space to a loft conversion or newly built urban apartment, the style is quite different. This is a classical version of

Halls in apartments are often dark, cramped, and cheerless spaces, with no natural light and no view. Thanks to a large window that opens onto a roof terrace at the top of the stairs, the entrance to this two-story, top-floor apartment is flooded with light from above. But Daniela Micol Wajskol has gone one better and given it yet more light and the bonus of views by carving wide archways that lead into the living room (FAR RIGHT) and dining room beyond. Paneling to dado level in the hall also wraps around the archways, linking the spaces visually and giving the new openings a look of permanence.

DECORATED IN PALE NEUTRALS AND OFF-WHITES, THE EFFECT IS TO MAXIMIZE SPACE AND LIGHT, GIVING A SUNNY ATMOSPHERE.

BELOW **The wide landing at the top of the stairs is lit by a wall of windows and a French door, which opens onto a roof terrace. This is all new space, a roof conversion on a grand scale, which has almost doubled the size of the apartment. Although the staircase is new, its simple, traditional design with slim metal banisters is timeless.**

open-plan. The arches have an almost Roman feel, and the architectural detailing is entirely in keeping with the age of the building, which dates from the early twentieth century. Even the banisters, slim rods of metal with a simple ball finial, are a modern take on a traditional design.

Furnishings are similarly graceful and restrained; an antique console with a perfectly symmetrical arrangement of lamps and pots and, at the entrance to the living room, a painted metal urn on a stone pedestal. Modern twists like the basketweave lampshades and the sculptural orchid in the urn add to the sophistication of the scheme. Wall and ceiling light fixtures are decorative as well as functional. The simple glass cylinder of the ceiling light is supplemented by a row of charming wall lights made in metal with crystal drops to Daniela's design.

Upstairs, Daniela allowed space for a wide landing, from which a door opens onto the terrace. Decorated throughout in pale neutrals and off-whites, the whole effect is to maximize space and light, giving the apartment an airy, sunny atmosphere.

THIS PAGE Polished oak flooring, stained a warm nut brown, has been used throughout the apartment and continues up the staircase and onto the landing. The hall table holds a typically symmetrical arrangement of lamps and pots, given a twist by the unusual woven wicker lampshades. The mirror is a practical furnishing for a hall—just the place to check the angle of your hat—and here reflects the views from the living-room windows. The metal wall lights with crystal drops (OPPOSITE. ABOVE) are Daniela's design.

BEDROOMS

Bedrooms have a special and very personal status. If you were lucky enough as a child to have your own bedroom, you will remember that safe and satisfying feeling as you shut the door behind you for a good read, or a good cry, or a secret conversation with your best friend. In a house full of other people, your bedroom was a retreat and a refuge. As adults, a private bedroom that offers a sense of security as you sleep is just as important. Even in the open-plan acreage of a loft conversion, our instinct is to protect our beds with screens or half walls or curtains. Comfort is paramount—a bed you can relax in, curtains or blinds that shut out the sun, and a bedside light that you can switch on or off without having to emerge from under the quilt. And because the bedroom is essentially a private space, it can also be one in which we indulge our decorative whims.

RIGHT **Modern clothes require modern storage. The clothes hanger wasn't invented until the turn of the last century, before which time clothes were hung on hooks or folded in chests. Clare Mosley has incorporated hanging and shelf space on each side of the chimney breast, masked by the plain paneling that covers the whole wall.**
BELOW **A cushion in rich purple velvet picks up one of the less prominent colors from the chintz and drops a dollop of luxurious texture into the tracery of pattern.**

GEORGIAN REVISITED Quiet colors, antique furniture, and a striking chinoiserie chintz make a bedroom that is a haven of period charm, while bypassing inconveniences of the past.

When designer-craftswoman Clare Mosley bought her Georgian row house in London, it was a riot of 1970s kitsch. "In a way it was rather wonderful," she remembers, "but we decided to strip it back and restore its period feel, without compromising comfort." The main bedroom has all the elegance of a room dating from 1795, when the house was built, plus the more contemporary conveniences of wall-to-wall carpet, closets, a king-sized bed, and a connecting bathroom.

The decorative starting point for the room was the canopied Directoire bed, which Clare and her husband bought while living in France. The bed had tattered hangings, which Clare replaced with a new French fabric by Le Manach, in an eighteenth-century chinoiserie design. Double beds of this period are almost always much smaller than modern beds. While this bed was fortunately long enough, it was too narrow, so they extended it beyond the width of the head- and footboards. The expansion doesn't spoil the look of the bed, but makes it useable.

The two sash windows with their sliding shutters were intact, but the original fireplace had been taken out. Clare decided not to reinstate it as it would use up too much valuable wall space in a room that is not particularly large. Instead, she used the alcoves on each side of the chimney breast as closet space. To

THIS PICTURE The color of the walls and woodwork is one of those infinitely subtle shades that defies a single-word description, hovering somewhere between palest blue or smoky green, and dusty gray. It was a color Clare knew already from faded eighteenth-century painted furniture, but as it did not exist on any commercial paint chart, she had it mixed specially by Papers and Paints. And, because it is a pale, shadowy color, it works to make the room look larger. The door leads through to the bathroom.

STORAGE *A single, freestanding armoire rarely provides enough storage for the clothes we own. Clare has supplemented this piece with hidden storage on each side of the original chimney breast on the opposite wall.*

CANOPY *The antique French bed came complete with its canopy, which has been rehung with a document chintz. A canopy makes any bed look grand and imposing, and works particularly well when the bed is placed centrally, as here.*

WALLS *Clare used a specially commissioned shade of powdery blue-gray for the walls and the woodwork. Making no color distinction between door frames, doors, baseboards, and the walls between them has the effect of expanding space.*

FLOORING *The original boards were uneven and damaged. Instead Clare chose a carpet in a shade of mink gray as shadowy as the walls. Again, the encompassing neutral color magnifies space, while the softness muffles sound and makes the room cozy.*

FURNITURE *The room contains few but elegant pieces of antique furniture, mostly eighteenth century, although the chest of drawers is 1930s. All are united by a simplicity that is appropriate to the modest Georgian proportions of the room.*

DOORWAYS *The house retained its original four-paneled doors. Clare added a second door to her bedroom to lead into the bathroom. It matches and balances the door from the landing, which is to the left of the bed.*

ABOVE AND BELOW **This room contains strong pattern in the chintz (2) (which is also used for the shades), and some highly decorative objects such as the carved mirror and the decalcomania glass jars and lamp bases, which Clare embellishes with flowers and gilding. This decorative** richness is carefully deployed and contrasted with the plain walls in flat latex (1) and the plain carpet, just as the chintz on the bed contrasts with the plain velvet pillow (3). Decorative objects are large and few, and arranged with formal symmetry on the desk and, here, on the chest of drawers. **There are no small knickknacks or fussy details, with the result that the room seems calm and poised, rather than busy.** ABOVE RIGHT **The bathroom echoes the colors of the bedroom in a faded toile de Jouy that covers the sofa and a wallpaper that depicts scenes of fishing.**

keep the effect as simple and seamless as possible, she paneled the whole wall, incorporating the closet doors in the paneling and taking the cupboards up to the ceiling to maximize storage.

In between the cupboards, where the fireplace would have been, she has placed an antique desk, with a poised arrangement of two of her own-design decalcomania jars and an inlaid box on its top, and a picture hung over it. Because the proportions of the desk are similar to those of the original fireplace, it takes the place of the fireplace, providing a central focus for the end wall of the room.

Opposite the bed Clare has matched an eighteenth-century French mirror with a 1930s chest of drawers. Placing a mirror, or pier glass as they were called, between windows was a favorite decorative device in the eighteenth century. The mirror throws extra light back into the room, and the soft reflection of the silvered glass adds depth and an illusion of space.

Although Clare has mixed furnishings from different periods, three of the most prominent pieces, the bed, chest of drawers, and mirror, are linked by the gentle shades of their slightly distressed paint finishes. In order to achieve exactly the right powdery gray-blue she envisaged for the walls and woodwork, Clare had a paint specially mixed for her by Papers and Paints. The color binds the other neutral shades in the room, including the minky gray of the velvet carpet. By choosing not to pick out the windows, baseboards, and doors in another shade, Clare has pared down the decorative scheme to an elegant simplicity and made the room seem bigger.

Against this background of soft, "knocked-back" color, the strawberry red and brown of the chintz bed hangings and window treatments make a strong decorative statement. Rather than overdo the effect with yards of curtain, Clare chose more modest shades.

LEFT **Roman shades in pure, unlined linen have a generous border of pale mushroom and are an exact match with the bedlinen.** BELOW **Nothing makes a bed look more inviting** than leaving a selection of plump pillows on show, even though not hiding them beneath a bedspread means you may have to iron them a little more carefully than you would otherwise.

ITALIAN MADE SIMPLE

In a compact bedroom in Milan, down pillows, linen, and well-chosen furniture combine for comfort and style.

The main bedroom of Daniela Micol Wajskol's Milan apartment is not a particularly large room. It has a high ceiling and a single tall window, and space for not much more than the French-size double bed. Nevertheless, the impression is of a room of generous proportions, and this is largely due to Daniela's careful choice of colors and furnishings.

As is so often the case with a successful room, it is not so much what has been included as what has been excluded that counts. Aside from the bed and the pair of neat, modern bedside tables, made in pergamena wood, there is a giltwood antique bergère, a slim-legged stool, an early nineteenth-century mahogany secretaire, and nothing else.

Each of these pieces of furniture is as beautiful as it is useful. Single chairs are oddly invaluable in bedrooms, not so much for sitting on as for draping once-worn sweaters or the clothes you plan to wear the next day. The long stool at the end of the bed has a similar role; a place to put things down. But it can also be pulled over so that Daniela can sit at the secretaire. This refined antique, with its classical columns and rich patina, provides a surface for family photographs and drawers for clothes, and incorporates a door that folds down to make a desk or dressing table, revealing smaller drawers ideal for storing cosmetics. As for the bedside tables, we all know how hard it is to manage without them.

One of the problems when furnishing a bedroom is inevitably how to provide enough storage for the vast wardrobe of clothes most of us own today. Antique pieces rarely suffice as the rod jangling with hangers is a relatively modern development, which only took over from hooks and chests at the end of the nineteenth century. Built-in closets are by far the most efficient use of space, but often look ugly and domineering, especially in smaller rooms.

THE SOFT LILAC-GRAY OF THE BEDSPREAD IS PICKED UP IN THE LINEN ROMAN SHADES, WHICH FILTER THE GLARE OF THE ITALIAN SUN.

THIS PICTURE Calm muted colors like these are particularly appropriate for a bedroom, as relaxing for the eye as the bed promises to be for the body. Also visually soothing is the balance between symmetry and asymmetry—strict symmetry can make a room feel too formal. Here, although the pillows and bedside tables present perfect symmetry, the table lamps and the bright pink orchid interfere.

Daniela's solution was to fill a whole wall of her bedroom with floor-to-ceiling built-in closets, but to break their monotony with an alcove into which the secretaire fits perfectly. This gives the closets an architectural feel, which is reinforced by the way the shallow fielded paneling of the doors continues on the back wall of the alcove and the narrow molding that tops the closets follows around the ceiling.

Colors in this room are calm and muted. Below the dado rail the walls are sponged in flat pearl gray, the same color as the closet doors. The remainder of the walls are ivory, an off-white that perfectly matches the linen of the sheets and pillowcases. Breaking the walls up horizontally into two areas of color helps to make a relatively small, high-ceilinged room such as this seem less tall and thin. The soft lilac-gray of the bedspread is picked up in the borders of the linen Roman shades, which filter the blinding glare of the Italian sun. External shutters are closed at night.

The only dark colors in this room of creams and grays are the glossy dark browns of the secretaire and the floorboards, which are also antique. Although newly built, this old floor gives the room a real air of permanence and period style.

Daniela Micol Wajskol designs particularly elegant built-in closets, an aesthetic challenge that is more difficult than it sounds. In this room she has filled a whole wall with two-tier hanging space, but has broken the row of doors with an alcove into which an antique secretaire fits snugly. By continuing the beaded molding of the doors on the wall at the back of the alcove and by framing it with a shaped valance, she has made an attractive architectural feature of an often unsightly bedroom necessity. The pearly gray of the paint, which covers the walls up to the dado, is also used on the closets and makes a subtle foil for the dark glow of the antique wooden floor and the secretaire. The pretty eighteenth-century chair (LEFT) is charmingly silhouetted in the window.

THIS PICTURE In a room as bright and white and empty as this, the powerful purple curves of the Tongue chair jump out like a spotlit sculpture in an art gallery. In fact, the room is far from all white, a choice that would have been blinding in a space with so much light. The huge bed is clothed in shades of cream with a linen dust ruffle and headboard, and the alcove in which it sits is painted the gray of gentle shadow. Also creamy, as opposed to white, are the limestone floor and the tufted linen rug, which forms an island of soft texture all around the bed. In addition to a view of trees and grass, the bedroom has a view through a glass panel into the bathroom and beyond (OPPOSITE).

ROOM WITH A VIEW Surrounded by garden and mature trees, and with a view through huge picture windows into the distance over a golf course, this bedroom and bathroom in a 1960s house barely needed the visual distraction of furniture.

The main bedroom and bathroom of this 1960s house create an enfilade across its back elevation with a view of trees that stretches far into the distance over the garden to the golf course beyond. Huge floor-to-ceiling picture windows march along the back wall, and there are also windows at each corner, allowing a lateral view from the roof terrace right through the bedroom and through an internal window into the bathroom and garden.

When architect Fiona McLean remodeled the house, she recognized this wraparound vista as the greatest strength of the space and set about maximizing its impact. Furnishings in the bedroom are few but deeply luxurious. The huge but otherwise modest bed, with its chaste cream and white bed linen, is purportedly the most comfortable bed that money can buy. To make it feel more integral to the design of the room, Fiona built out the walls on each side of it to create a shallow alcove. The back wall of the alcove is painted a receding, shadowy gray, giving an illusion of greater depth.

The remainder of the walls are white, the floor is pale limestone, and the rug, which offers a pool of

softness around the bed, is creamy linen. Because
there is a walk-in closet next to the bathroom, there
is no need for much other furniture. The bedside
tables are simple and practical, and hold a pair of
lamps with snowy white shades. Wit and a jolt of
color and pattern are injected into this serene setting
by the royal purple Tongue chair and a three-legged
modern chest of drawers (not shown), which is
veneered in stripy zebrano wood. Beyond these
bold, decorative touches, there is little to distract
from the tracery of branches and tapestry of green
framed by the windows.

There is a small step up from the bedroom to the
bathroom, a difference in floor level that allowed
pipes and the support for the vanity unit to be
hidden. The limestone flooring in the bathroom
is a slightly darker shade. But the large window
between the rooms, to the right of the sliding door,
not only affords an uplifting view, it makes the two
spaces feel linked and open.

The view from the window is naturally beautiful,
but the bathroom is arranged such that the view of it

from the bedroom is also aesthetically pleasing; a T-shaped, limestone-covered podium, upon which are balanced a pair of shallow cast glass basins made by Jeff Bell, each with an impossibly elegant single faucet arching over it. The traps for the basins are enclosed in the central column so it looks as if they are freestanding, translucent bowls, more decorative than useful. A half-squeezed tube of toothpaste or bar of soggy soap would ruin this sculptural purity. Disciplined owners keep them hidden behind the mirrored glass doors of the pair of floor-to-ceiling cabinets. A sliding door can be pulled across to separate bed- and bathroom.

Opposite the basins are a shower and toilet, both screened by acid-etched glass walls. In between is the ultimate in sybaritic bathing; a semi-sunken bath, lined with smooth honed granite and heated from below. Privacy is secondary to the view (the house is surrounded by its own yard), but when modesty or insecurity triumph or at night when the house is lit up and the garden is dark, there are electronically controlled blinds, which descend to the floor at the press of a button.

FAR LEFT **A window to the left of the bed looks out onto the second-floor roof terrace.**
LEFT **Looking back into the bedroom from the bathroom, you can see right through this window and across the whole width of the back of the house, thanks to a wall of glass between the bedroom and bathroom. This particular view is complicated by the column of mirror glass that fronts the cabinet standing between the bathroom door and the internal window. The effect is of endless vistas stretching ahead, and reflected from behind, maximizing the great strength of these plain, modernist spaces. It feels like being inside a transparent, sheltering box set in the middle of a woodland copse. Being in suburbia however, and not the middle of the country, privacy is an issue. Crisp Roman blackout shades in the bedroom and the bathroom** (BELOW RIGHT) **are electronically controlled.**
ABOVE RIGHT **A detail of one of the cast glass basins.**

A SHIP OF DREAMS Most of us, as children, have imagined our bed as a boat. Architect and designer Wizam Kamleh made that dream come true.

Children have notoriously fickle tastes. One day pink is their favorite color, and everything pink from ice cream to the carpet is utterly lovely. And then, suddenly, they hate pink, and woe betide you if you have painted their room in this dreadful color.

This stunning bedroom with its boat bed and fishy mural was designed for a four-year-old girl who, when consulted, insisted that boats were her favorite thing. Designer Wizam Kamleh took her at her word and made the most perfect boat-lover's bedroom you could wish for. Five months later, however, boats were no longer the little girl's favorite thing. But fortunately this change of heart did not dampen her enthusiasm for her new room.

Themed bedrooms for children are just as exciting a project for the designer as they are for the child, and provide a unique opportunity to experiment and to let the imagination run wild, free from the usual worries that you might be thought tasteless or weird. However, it is equally important that the room should be practical, with as much storage as you can squeeze in, and that it should be adaptable. The only themes most teenagers are interested in are played on synthesizers and electric guitars.

Wizam Kamleh's boat bedroom fulfills all these requirements. The boat has been designed around a standard mattress and could be transformed from childhood fantasy to something more sophisticated with a coat of paint. The steps that lead up to the bed contain three large storage drawers, and there is space in the room for other furnishings, a desk, a bookcase, a computer, a stereo, as the child grows up.

The boat was constructed with a supporting base of studwork and plywood slats wrapped around composite-board ribs. The design was drawn on a computer, and templates made for cutting the wood. The metal rail, from a nautical supplier, is authentic.

One of the reasons this room works so well is because the colorful boat and busy mural are set in a room that is otherwise entirely plain. This home is carved out of an old printworks in London and still has an industrial feel. The ceiling is concrete and other walls are painted flat white. There are no baseboards or other architectural details, just a metal-framed window and an inner window of rectangular glass bricks that admits light to the kitchen next door.

Wizam made an initial sketch for the mural and handed it over to a mural painter to be translated onto the walls and boat. The style is graphic and bold, and avoids the tweeness and sentimentality that so often infect murals in children's rooms.

There is a wall light just above the prow of the bed for nighttime reading, and for sheer prettiness, and ambient light, there are four recessed halogen lights with starbursts painted around them. Wizam used cabinet lights, which have a very shallow fixture and could be set into the depth of the plaster.

The finished room is a delight. One day, the little girl may tire of her painted crabs and seaweed, but there is every chance she will keep her boat bed until she leaves home and is ready to design her own room.

RIGHT **This bright, witty scheme was designed for a little girl who loved boats, its central feature a bed cleverly constructed from composite board and plywood to look like the prow of a sailing ship cutting through the waves. Spending large amounts of money on a themed bedroom can be a mistake if the design is not flexible enough to grow with the child and his or her tastes. The beauty of this room is that it is sophisticated enough not to embarrass an older child and, if necessary, could be painted all white and still look stylish enough for a teenager.**
TOP LEFT **The little halogen lights, which make the painted stars twinkle, are cabinet lights with shallow fixtures that were recessed into the plaster.**
BELOW **The steps up to the bed provide storage for clothes and toys.**

THE STYLE IS GRAPHIC AND BOLD, AND AVOIDS THE TWEENESS AND
SENTIMENTALITY THAT SO OFTEN INFECT MURALS IN CHILDREN'S ROOMS.

LEFT The boat was constructed around the dimensions of a single-bed mattress, making this a bed that would fit a teenager as well as it does a small child. The railings were sourced from a nautical supply store and add a certain authenticity, while also preventing the bed's occupant from falling overboard and keeping all those teddy bears safely on deck.

THIS PAGE Ample storage is essential in any child's bedroom. The design of the boat bed, raised high above floor level and reached by wooden steps, allows space for capacious drawers in the wooden platform beneath.

SWEET AND SWEDISH
Moussie Sayers brought her own brand of pretty Nordic style to the bedroom of her Edwardian house and made it look "twice the size and twice as light."

A color scheme of yellow, blue, and white always looks fresh and wholesome. In this bedroom, the yellow has been toned down to a shade of palest primrose; the white of walls, furniture, and woodwork is a soft off-white, and the blue is the deep, rich indigo of old Delft pottery. This makes the color combination more subtle and sophisticated without losing any of its freshness. Four fabrics, all of which coordinate, are used repeatedly. A copy of an eighteenth-century toile (2, overleaf) covers the headboard, upholsters the chair, and makes window shades in the bedroom and curtains in the bathroom. Its companion toile (3), a smaller pattern in the same colors, covers pillows on the bed, and lines the shades. Closets are hung with gathered voile in dark blue gingham (1), and the same cream voile hangs as curtains at the bedroom window and from the corona above the bed.

In the kitchens section of this book, you can see how designer Moussie Sayers interpreted eighteenth-century Swedish Gustavian style to suit cooking and eating in a modern home. In her bedroom and bathroom, the same style takes on a more formal elegance. "But it's still very practical," she insists. "All the fabrics are easy to take down and all are washable."

The color scheme of the room combines an exceptionally gentle pale yellow with the indigo blue and cream of the toile she has used for the shades in the bedroom, the curtains in the bathroom, and to upholster chairs and the headboard. The design of the toile is a direct copy of an eighteenth-century original, a fresh, simple pattern of flowers and ribbons. Taking another cue from the past, she has used its companion fabric, a toile in the same colors with a tighter, smaller pattern of stripes and sprigs, to cover pillows on the bed and to line the shades. The two fabrics complement one another perfectly, just as they were originally designed to do.

Picking up on the blue and cream of the toile is the gingham voile Moussie used to screen the closet doors. The closets, which are built in and stretch from floor to ceiling along one wall of the room, were already in place. Moussie adapted them to her own style by cutting out stepped panels in the doors. The heavily gathered voile is attached to rods on the inside of the doors so it can be unhooked and washed. The effect is pretty and a clever way to lighten and break up the expanse of doors, which can overpower a room of this size.

RIGHT AND FAR RIGHT
The bathroom that leads off the bedroom uses exactly the same color scheme and some of the same fabric. The original floorboards sweep from one room into the next, although there is a raised platform of painted wooden flooring next to the bathtub, to hide the pipes.
LEFT A detail of the closet doors, which have been dragged with an "antique" glaze. The voile curtains that fill the cut-out door panels are attached to rods inside the doors so they can be easily removed and washed. All the fabrics used in this room are washable, which is particularly important in a London bedroom where grime always finds its way inside, even when the windows are firmly closed.

Instead, the room is dominated by the bed, which makes a far more comfortable and appealing focus. The corona above the bed, which emphasizes its status in the room, is typically restrained, allowing a fall of fabric against the wall to make a backdrop for the headboard. Again Moussie has chosen voile for its lightness and freshness, this time in plain creamy white. The same plain voile is hung at the windows as outer curtains, which soften the edges of the windows but are not designed to be drawn. Behind these are shades, which can be lowered for privacy as well as being decorative, and behind these shades are hidden blackout blinds for use on summer nights.

In her kitchen Moussie used pale colors to increase the sense of light. Here she adds mirrors to reflect even more light; a large, framed wall mirror in the bedroom and sheets of mirror glass framed with wooden beadings in the adjoining bathroom. This much smaller room continues the decorative theme of the bedroom with the same plain, varnished floorboards, the same soft white paintwork and the same toile at the window. Painted tongue and groove match-boarding panels the walls and makes a platform next to the bathtub under which the pipework runs.

Finishing touches include candles in antique and reproduction candlesticks in both bedroom and bathroom, providing light for bathing and bedtime that is just as romantic as it is for dining.

CANDLES IN ANTIQUE AND REPRODUCTION CANDLESTICKS PROVIDE A LIGHT FOR BATHING AND BEDTIME THAT IS JUST AS ROMANTIC AS IT IS FOR DINING.

BATHROOMS

Have you ever noticed how when anyone is describing a particularly luxurious hotel they will always rhapsodize about the bathroom—the huge tub, the fluffy towels, the walk-in shower, the bottles of scented oils and lotions. Expensive hotels are an indulgence, their bathrooms the epitome of indulgence. Bathrooms offer an escape even more private than the bedroom. Here you can sing out of tune while pummeled by your power shower, lie and read in a bath of bubbles until the book gets soggy, or simply spend more time than strictly necessary washing your face and peering in the mirror. Needless to say, a bathroom must be practical, the plumbing needs to work, the ventilation must be good, the floor and walls should be water-resistant. But with careful design your own bathroom can also evoke some of that luxury you would otherwise have to pay through the nose for.

THE LARGEST ROOM A bathroom that is too big sounds like
an asset to be proud of, but although you won't have to resort to a shower in the
bathtub, it can pose almost as many design problems as one that is too small.

Interior designer Helen Ellery describes the original layout of this giant bathroom as looking like a photo booth in a train station. "It's such a big room," she says, "and yet everything was all squashed together in a corner. It looked dreadful and made you feel uncomfortably exposed."

Space is always a luxury, and yet as Helen points out, the arrangement and scale of bathroom fixtures in a room this size have to be carefully considered. A small single washbasin or little teeny bathtub would look silly and lost here. Helen's solution was to source a very large refurbished antique bathtub, which she placed firmly in the middle of the room, and an opulent double basin, which she installed in

the center of the original chimney breast. And, making the most of the generous floor space, she filled the corner of the room on the right of the chimney breast with a huge, walk-in shower that is so big it doesn't even need doors.

Instead of the old floorboards, which were uneven and in bad condition, Helen decided to put in a limestone floor, giving a cool contemporary edge to the classical Georgian architecture of the room. "People think you can't put stone floors upstairs in old houses," she comments. "We did have to renew the joists, but aside from that, it was not a problem. Modern stone floors come as slim tiles, and the weight is very evenly spread. We put down a layer of

Even the grandest Georgian houses were built without bathrooms, meaning that either a former bedroom must be partitioned to create bathroom space or, as in this house, given over in its entirety to the modern essentials of bathtub, toilet, basins, and shower. Modern bathrooms can look very stylish in the setting of period architecture, but Helen Ellery has chosen more traditional fixtures that hark back to the Edwardian era, when bathrooms as we know them today were first being installed.

WINDOW TREATMENTS
White Roman shades are in keeping with the clean simplicity of the room. The plain fabric is embroidered with life-size nudes, making them look like giant pen-and-ink sketches when lowered.

WALLS *To break up the expanse of wall in a room of such grand proportions, Helen added fielded paneling to dado level to match the paneling of the shutters and window recesses. It is painted soft sage green and the walls cream.*

BASIN *In a room this large, small fixtures would look lost. Helen found a double washbasin supported on molded legs, which has all the presence of a grand piece of furniture. Faucets and fixtures are also suitably chunky.*

BATHTUB *Placing all the bathroom fixtures around the edge of this room would have left a huge expanse of floor space completely empty. Instead a massive, reconditioned antique bathtub takes center stage.*

FLOORING *The room has a crisp, clean feel, which is largely due to the pale limestone tiles that have taken the place of floorboards. They are laid over marine plywood, and underfloor heating has been installed.*

SHOWER *With no shortage of space to limit its design, the shower fills one whole corner of the room and is capacious enough not to need a door. One side of it is boxed in with a wall, which continues the paneling and has a glass screen on top.*

LEFT **The bathroom leads straight off the main bedroom, and the door through allows a vista of the four high sash windows. Colors in both rooms are carefully coordinated. The bedroom has curtains in mauve toile de Jouy with a deep border of purple velvet, and the carpet is also mauve. The combination of these colors with the green of the bathroom is fresh and pretty, and reminds Helen of lilac and wisteria.**

THE SOFT SAGE GREEN OF THE BATHROOM WOODWORK GIVES A FRESH, GARDEN FEEL, EMPHASIZED BY THE HUGE POTTED FERN.

marine plywood as a base, and there was even space for underfloor heating, which makes the room feel warm and welcoming however cold it is outside."

Even the most generous bathroom fixtures are inevitably low level, and this is emphasized in a room with high ceilings. To break up the vertical plane of the walls, Helen designed fielded paneling, which lines the walls to dado level and which exactly matches the paneling of the window shutters. "Many of the other rooms in the house have original eighteenth-century paneling," she explains, "so it seemed particularly appropriate." The new paneling, in painted composite, also extends around the wall of the shower, and helps make it feel a structural part of the room as opposed to an incongruous add-on.

Lighting is discreet and focused; a series of recessed ceiling spotlights with halogen bulbs. There are also two floor-mounted halogen lights underneath the tub. "When these are the only lights in the room, it creates a very soothing atmosphere, and the bath almost looks as though it is floating," says Helen.

The room leads directly through from the main bedroom, which is decorated in shades of purple. The soft sage green of the bathroom woodwork complements these colors perfectly and gives the two rooms a fresh, garden feel, emphasized by the huge potted fern that sits on one windowsill. "I like to try to bring the outdoors inside when I am decorating," says Helen, "and these colors remind me of lilac and wisteria."

Decorative touches are few and restrained; engraved glass bottles on shelves and another potted plant. There are no pictures on the walls, but there are two graceful nudes sketched in embroidery on the linen Roman shades. The design is simple and large scale, a modern decorative style that sits well within the elegant proportions of this grand Georgian room.

ABOVE **A second door leads out of the bathroom onto the landing. The bath is centrally placed in a room that demands a certain symmetry. Set into the floor beneath it are two uplighters, which make the tub look like an eerily floating white boat when they are the only lights on in a darkened room.**
LEFT **The design of the bathtub, unlike the more usual "rolltop," allows space for putting things, like these engraved glass bottles into which favorite bath oils can be decanted.**

THE ABUNDANCE OF NATURAL LIGHT AND THE LACK
OF WINDOWS MAKE THE ROOM FEEL ENCLOSED AND
PRIVATE WITHOUT BEING CLAUSTROPHOBIC.

PLAIN BEAUTY The chaste simplicity of this bathroom in a Long Island house gives it a contemplative, almost monastic atmosphere, the perfect place to relax and meditate far from city life.

When interior designer Kelly Behun and her husband bought a weekend house on Long Island, they were determined that it should be an antidote to their busy working weeks in the city. The house is a plain wooden one-story building, but its previous decoration was cluttered and glitzy. The bathroom, which leads off the main bedroom, was awash with glossy marble and spiked with shiny gold faucets.

"We decorated this room last," Kelly remembers. "We had done the rest of the house very simply, and I wanted this to be the ultimate chill-out room, somewhere to linger and decompress." Kelly chose a creamy limestone from Wisconsin, with very even coloring, to tile the floor, form the baseboards, line the shower, support the basin, and form the bathtub. The effect is of soothing uniformity.

The room had been designed as a bathroom when the house was built, so there was already space for underfloor plumbing. Kelly also installed underfloor heating, making sure the limestone is warm underfoot when the weather is cold. The floor runs straight into the shower, with only the smallest bevel to discourage water from flowing out, but the base of the shower is subtly angled toward the drain.

The biggest technical challenge was constructing the bathtub. Kelly wanted it to look as though it rose from the floor in one solid, monolithic block. Fortunately she found a craftsman skilled enough to create the illusion using mitered slabs of limestone.

Inside the tub Kelly installed a teak backrest so she can lie back at an angle against the straight stone walls.

One of the special qualities the room possessed was the light, which pours down from two large square skylights. The abundance of natural light and the lack of windows make the room feel enclosed and private without being claustrophobic. Kelly installed two very large mirrors to reflect this top light and spread it more evenly around the room. The mirror above the basin is mounted invisibly a few inches out from the wall so it looks as though it is floating, while the mirror behind the bathtub, which Kelly had framed in dark wood to match the stool, is propped rather than hung.

Achieving such perfect simplicity is never as easy as it might look. Maintaining it requires strict self-discipline. Beneath the washbasin are two wicker baskets. These are the only storage in the room, the top one containing things used often, such as soap and toothpaste, the bottom one holding lesser essentials. "I realized I was prone to keeping a lot of things I don't really need," says Kelly. "I decided I wanted to be rigorous in this house. I don't live like that in the city, but here, I really enjoy it."

FAR LEFT **The clean rectangle of the limestone bathtub has the proportions of an altar and rises from the floor, which is tiled in the same pale stone, as if carved from the same monolithic block as the floor itself. It sits directly beneath one of two square skylights, and yet more light is reflected from the huge mirror behind it and the mirror over the washbasin.**
ABOVE **The ceramic basin in the shape of a shallow bowl sits on another slab of limestone. Even the faucets are pared down to the essential of a single curving pipe.**
LEFT **The faucet for the bath, a single arched pipe, was designed specially for the room by Kelly and is controlled from a discreet knob set into the wall.**

ABOVE A stone bathtub, as any Roman would tell you, is surprisingly comfortable because of the way stone absorbs and retains heat. Kelly added a teak backrest to her stone tub so she can lie back and soak.

LEFT Kelly wanted the room to have an organic feel and has filled woven baskets with a selection of natural sponges.

FAR LEFT The shower is also lined in limestone. The tray is very subtly angled toward a central drain.

Although this bathroom
is uncompromisingly
contemporary, there are
elements of its design that
refer back to bathing rituals
from long ago, such as the
use of stone for the bathtub
and the bowl-shaped basin.
This sits on top of a stone
surface in an echo of the
jug and basin that stood on
the washstand of every
Victorian bedroom. The
orange lilies and the warm,
buttery yellow of the
sponges introduce color
and softness into a room
that takes its character
from the smooth solidity
of pale stone.

LEFT **In a bathroom that uses materials particularly innovatively, a whole wall behind the twin washbasins is paneled with two huge sheets of glass, acid etched and sealed except for two perfect circles that have been left with their mirror backing intact, making it look as if two round moons of reflection have been wiped clean of mist. The sheets join horizontally at the same height as the basins, so the eye barely notices the seam.**
RIGHT AND BELOW **Bath and shower fixtures are sleek, modern, and minimal.**

PERFECTLY MATCHED A rare
mix of "ideal clients" and a building with plenty of space and scope for imagination allowed Clinton Pritchard to create a bathroom to be proud of.

It isn't often that an interior designer is offered a genuinely blank canvas. Usually there are a whole raft of constraints, from the shape and size of a room to the taste and budget of the client. Clinton Pritchard of Zynk Design Consultants came close to perfect design freedom when he was commissioned by David Vanderhook. The result is 2,500 square feet (230 square meters) of innovative modern living where David, who is a chef and entrepreneur, and his wife Joanna, both live and work.

They bought the space as a shell. The lower ground floor, which is below sidewalk level, had some small windows and skylights, but was otherwise featureless. There was enough floor space to carve out six bedrooms with their own bathrooms. But instead of dividing it into boxes, Clinton persuaded David and Joanna to make the most of its greatest asset, openness, and add as few inner walls as practical. What has been lost in quantity of rooms has been amply repaid in their quality. The master bathroom is four times the size of most and incorporates a walk-in shower big enough to hold a small party in.

The brief for the bathroom was simple; enough elbow room for two people rushing to get ready in the morning, enough storage so toothbrushes, cotton swabs, and toilet cleaner needn't be on show, and a generous shower. The rest was up to Clinton Pritchard's imagination and ingenuity.

RIGHT **Glass clothes one wall, and a geometrical jigsaw of zebrano wood covers another wall behind the bathtub. The striking grain of this tropical hardwood has been cross-matched, and each panel is strongly outlined by shadow where the wall behind is painted dark brown. Good looks aside, the panels have also been arranged so that some of them lift out to give access to critical parts of the plumbing. A heated towel rod is mounted directly on the panels.**

ARCHITECTURE *The bathroom is on the lower ground floor of a former printworks, bought as a shell. This gave Clinton Pritchard the freedom to build it the exact shape and size he wanted. As it is an internal room, there were not even windows to be accommodated.*

PLUMBING *The floor was raised to allow space for pipework, and the wall behind the bathtub is a dummy wall in which the support plumbing services are buried. On the far side of this wall is a utility room, which also takes advantage of the hidden plumbing.*

FLOORING *The floor is tiled in ceramic mosaic tiles 1 in (2.5 cm) square in dark chocolate brown. The color was chosen as an alternative to black, because it has the same decorative effect but soaks up less light.*

MATERIALS *This is a room that uses materials in unusual and imaginative ways, particularly glass, which covers a whole wall and forms the shower. Even the Philippe Starck bathtub has been customized with a wrap of sheet aluminum over marine plywood.*

SHOWER *This is a technical as much as an aesthetic triumph and uses two enormous sheets of laminated curved glass, which protrude into the room beyond. The glass has been coated with the same water repellent that is used for aircraft windows.*

LEFT In between the washbasins is a capacious aluminum-sided cupboard, inside which are kept all those things that make a bathroom look messy. It also provides a surface for putting bottles, jars, and tubes that are in use.
BELOW A detail of the zebrano wood paneling and the slick bath faucets set into it. The extraordinary figured grain of the wood brings organic pattern into a room that might otherwise verge on the clinical.

BELOW Glass is a leitmotif in a room that graphically reveals what a versatile material it is. Thin sheets of glass, such as those used to cover the wall, must be glued to a flat surface for strength and rigidity, but thick glass, such as that used for the cast glass basins, is a surprisingly durable material, beautiful to look at and no more likely to chip than ceramic.

First came the practicalities. To provide good drainage, it being a basement room, the floor was raised by 1¼ in (3 cm). A false wall of zebrano wood paneling was installed at one end of the room, behind which the tank and pipework are hidden. The pattern of the paneling, which appears to have been designed on purely aesthetic grounds, has been carefully arranged to allow access to critical areas of the plumbing. Between the twin washbasins stands a large cabinet for hiding bathroom undesirables.

Fixtures are clean and modern. The giant bathtub with its plain rounded ends is by Philippe Starck, but it has been modified by Clinton Pritchard with a sleek wrap of aluminum. Faucets are Vola, by Arne Jacobsen, chosen for their "simple, geometric elegance." The pair of cast glass basins is by Duravit. Shower accessories are also Philippe Starck, but the shower itself, which is the real showstopper in the room, is pure Clinton Pritchard.

"Because this is an inner room," he explains, "I wanted to make the shower like a huge window." The curved walls of the shower are constructed from two giant glass panels, the largest such panels that can currently be manufactured, and they project from the bathroom into the space beyond. Translucent, rather than transparent, they incorporate a frosted layer laminated between two layers of clear glass. During the day they admit a greenish haze of borrowed daylight into the bathroom, while at night, when the shower is lit from within, the outside of the curved glass glows eerily.

Glass has been used in an equally innovative way as a waterproof wallcovering. Two very large sheets of mirror glass are glued to the wall behind the basins, the horizontal seam between them cunningly lined up with the top edge of the basins so the eye barely notices it. The mirror backing has been etched off except for two big circles over the basins where a round world of reflection appears seamlessly, as if from nowhere.

A WATERY RETREAT

Clare Mosley's bathroom is papered with river scenes while her bath alcove is paneled with *verre eglomise* mirror that shimmers like the surface of a lake.

Almost all houses that predate 1900 were built without bathrooms. This poses a dilemma in an age when multiple bathrooms, preferably one to serve each principal bedroom, are considered desirable, if not essential. The period house owner can either carve large bedrooms into smaller spaces to make extra bathrooms, usually ruining the proportions of a room in the process, or must sacrifice a bedroom.

Clare Mosley gave herself the luxury of converting a former bedroom in her Georgian townhouse to make a generous bathroom leading straight off the main bedroom. Far from seeming like a waste of valuable space, this is a bathroom you could happily live in; as much a room where you might retreat to read a book as a venue for the dreary rituals of teeth brushing and hair washing.

The temptation with a bathroom this size is to fill the space with lavish bathroom equipment; a huge central bath perhaps, twin washbasins, and a walk-in shower. In Clare's bathroom, however, these sanitary arrangements seem to take a back seat. Admittedly the tub is extra large, but it is placed against the wall and recessed in an alcove between cupboards, leaving the center of the room free. There is no separate shower, and the single washbasin is tucked in a corner next to the toilet. As a result, the room seems bigger, and there is space for that ultimate bathroom indulgence, a sofa, inviting bathtime conversation and promoting the idea that this is a room to linger in and enjoy.

The plain paneling of the cupboards on each side of the bathtub was designed to echo the paneling of the original sliding window shutters. On one side it encloses the hot water tank, and on the other a drying cupboard. Old-fashioned match-boarding behind the tub hides the pipework leading to the wall-mounted faucets.

Above the match-boarding are panels of Clare Mosley's handmade mirror glass, or *verre eglomise*. Backed with tissue-thin sheets of silver leaf, the mirror affords a soft and flattering reflection of both room and bather. Used to line a large area of wall, as

ABOVE **Detail of the shade in simple checked silk.**
RIGHT AND BELOW FAR RIGHT **The large bathtub with its central faucets is set into an alcove that has been created by two built-in cupboards on either side, one of which contains the hot water tank, the other space for towels and bed linen. Above a backsplash of painted match-boarding, which also serves to hide the pipework for the bath faucets, Clare has paneled the alcove with sheets of glass, which have been mirrored by the application of silver leaf, a technique known as *verre eglomise*. The reflection offered by this handcrafted mirror is blurred by the crackelure of the silver leaf and far more flattering than commercial mirror.**
ABOVE FAR RIGHT **To the left of the washbasin, gothic wall shelves hold a small library of novels, contributing to the sense that this a room for sitting around as well as for getting clean in.**

RIGHT AND FAR LEFT
Instead of putting a bathtub in the middle of the room, Clare has reserved pride of place for a pretty antique sofa. This one piece of furniture instantly transforms the room from a temple of hygiene to a boudoir where washing might be secondary to the more important business of relaxation. The toile that covers the sofa (2) introduces another busy pattern on top of the wallpaper (3), but it neither clashes nor competes because its colors are so gentle and faded, as are the colors of the checked silk (1) that has been used for the shades.
LEFT **A close-up of the eccentric wallpaper with its scenes of eighteenth-century fishermen, which gives the room such character. The backsplash of the washbasin is a sheet of clear glass, allowing the wallpaper to show through.**

here, mirror has the effect of increasing light, while also giving the illusion of added space. Clare has also mirror-paneled the sides of the bath alcove.

The most dramatic element of the decoration in this inviting and comfortable room is the gloriously eccentric wallpaper from Lewis and Wood, a suitably watery repeat of fishing scenes taken from an original eighteenth-century print. Although the coloring is a subtle palette of greens and browns, the crowded design with its trees, figures, houses, and clouds could be overpowering to the point of claustrophobia in a smaller room, or if used to cover all four walls. Here its effect is tempered by the comparative calm of the wall of painted and paneled cupboards and mirror.

Aside from the rich decorative flourishes of mirror and wallpaper, there is little in the way of ornament: no marble or tiles, no pillows on the sofa, no swags or drapes, just a checked silk shade at the window and plain carpet on the floor. The lack of clutter and the careful balance between the plain and the ornate make this a room of exceptional charm.

RIGHT The layout and design of this room all serve to emphasize its unusual shape. Washbasin, toilet, shower, second washbasin, and bathtub are all lined up against one wall, while the flooring forms three separate stripes. Even the doors at each end are oddly tall and narrow.

LONG STORY In a London bathroom that doubles as a fire-escape corridor, with slender proportions to match, length is emphasized and turned into a virtue.

Clever design can transform a problem into an asset. This long, thin bathroom in a London loft conversion is also a fire-escape corridor, bringing the apartment neatly into compliance with building regulations by allowing a passageway from the bedroom, which opens straight onto the living room and kitchen, to the entrance lobby.

"Translating buildings designed as factories into spaces that are domestic and enjoyable rather than just a visual statement is a real challenge," says architect David Mikhail. This apartment, sold as a shell, was deep rather than wide, with windows at each end and a dead space in the middle with very little natural light. Into this space has been slotted the bathroom-corridor, its floor raised one step up to accommodate plumbing, its ceiling a little lower than that in the rest of the apartment.

The top of this room, which sits along one side of the apartment like a slim box, houses fluorescent uplighters, which bounce light off the ceiling above it and spread a glow into the living room and kitchen.

Rather than apologize for the unusual proportions of the room, David Mikhail decided to accentuate its length, first by placing all the bathroom fixtures along one wall, but also by dividing the floor into three stripes of natural materials with strikingly different textures. The central, or circulation, zone,

ABOVE LEFT Only the mirror glass, which runs the length of the wall, works against the elongation of the room, giving the illusion from some angles that its width has been doubled. Beneath the mirror runs a long slot shelf, providing yet another horizontal line of perspective.
ABOVE The wooden flooring outside the shower is slatted, allowing excess water to drain into an extended shower tray.

limestone. Along the wall, shadow lines have been chiseled around the edges of each stone tile, and there is a long shelf slot at chest level, which holds soaps and lotions decanted into chic dispensers. Less good-looking bathroom essentials are stored in the sliding mirrored cupboards above.

This mirror glass continues through the glass shower cubicle and extends the length of the wall, creating a visual illusion from some angles that the room is twice its real width. The shower itself is virtually invisible when not in use. Closed in by two sheets of strengthened transparent glass mounted in sunken steel channels, the effect of being inside it is of taking a shower with no surrounding walls.

Above this side of the room the ceiling is lower. This allowed space for recessed downlighters and also for long-term storage in deep cupboards. Two powerful extractor fans mean that damp and condensation are never an issue.

THE SHOWER ITSELF IS VIRTUALLY INVISIBLE WHEN NOT IN USE. THE EFFECT IS OF TAKING A SHOWER WITH NO SURROUNDING WALLS.

which links the slightly elongated doors at each end, is oiled iroko wood. The boards in front of the shower cubicle have small gaps between them, allowing the water to drain into a specially made steel shower tray beneath. Against the original brick wall there is a strip of pebbles, loosely laid on a concrete base and surrounding a row of uplighters, which throw ellipses of light and draw the eye to the textures of the clay and mortar. The machined technology of the light fixtures makes a daring contrast with the natural scatter of stones, which look like a bit of beach that has found its way indoors. It's a dramatic effect and apparently not as impractical as you might think. The pebbles can be vacuumed safely, being too large and heavy to get sucked up into the vacuum cleaner.

The working zone of the room, which incorporates a generous bathtub, a shower, a toilet, and two washbasins, is characterized by flooring and paneling in slabs of a gray-green, honed Spanish

OPPOSITE **The shower barely intrudes into the enfilade of porcelain basins, toilet, and bathtub, as it has the same mirrored panel with shelf beneath as the rest of the wall and is enclosed on two sides by sheets of glass, which are recessed into the limestone floor in metal channels. The shower floor has been almost imperceptibly adjusted to allow water to drain between the limestone tiles as well as between the planks of the teak flooring. The mirrored panels above the washbasins slide aside to reveal shelving (OPPOSITE BELOW).**

ABOVE **A loose scattering of large pebbles makes a third stripe of flooring and adds a slightly disconcerting outdoors feel to this inner sanctum of a room. The natural colors and textures of the brick, the wood, and the stones are sharply countered by the metal** uplighters that line up along the wall, throwing ellipses of light across the brickwork.

LEFT **Washbasins are simple ceramic bowls mounted on slabs of the same limestone that tiles the floor, panels the walls, and surrounds the bathtub. Faucets are by Vola.**

WORK ROOMS

For most of the last century working from home was the preserve of the poorly paid piece-worker or the aristocratic estate owner. Today, thanks to the continual refinement of computer technology, it is a practical possibility in many types of career. If you work from home full time, a room that you can call your office is particularly important. In practical terms, you need somewhere to keep your papers, files, disks, and any other tools of your trade. Making a physical separation between work and the rest of your home life can also help to make this important separation on an emotional level. Even if you only work part time or occasionally at home, to have a study is to have somewhere to go where you can be your working self. Here you can shut the door, settle at your desk, and forget about the washing and the shopping and what you are going to cook for supper.

RIGHT **Daniela** has furnished her office with glamorous pieces of antique furniture that would look just as at home in a drawing room. In fact, the only clues that this is the headquarters of a successful, modern business are the computer on the desk and the wooden box files on the windowsill (ABOVE LEFT), which hold current design magazines for reference. Everything else, from disks to fax machines to printers and scanners and piles of swatches, is hidden behind closet doors. Even the desk lamp is elegant. Daniela finds the aesthetics of her working environment very important, and her first concern when designing this room was to provide enough good-looking storage, so she could hide the mess and mechanics that make most offices such a jumble. Neatness is even more important in a room that has to double as guest bedroom and evening television room (BELOW LEFT).

Interior designer Daniela Micol Wajskol's home office is characterized by refined antique furnishings and a brave, bold, bright shade of blue paint, the color of sky on a summer evening.

STUDY IN BLUE

Daniela Micol Wajskol's study has all the elegance of an eighteenth-century French boudoir. Her computer sits on an elaborate antique desk in cross-banded veneer with ormolu mounts. All other office effects, fabric swatches and samples, plus a television and stereo, are hidden behind the doors of two capacious cupboards. The wall opposite the desk is covered by floor-to-ceiling book shelving, and current issues of design magazines are stored in wooden box files on the windowsills.

Daniela chose one of the larger bedrooms in her Milan apartment as the office from which to run her interior design business. But this was not an entirely selfish choice, since the room has other functions beyond the demands of work. This is also a second living room where the whole family watches television and listens to music. And without its liberal padding of bolsters and cushions, the sofa becomes a divan and the room is transformed into a guest bedroom.

The great attraction of this room is the way in which it sidesteps the ugliness that so often goes hand in hand with modern efficiency. The leather-topped desk is perfectly practical but also a fine piece of furniture. The antique chair, upholstered in a copy of an eighteenth-century chintz, is as pretty as it is comfortable. The only piece of plastic-wrapped technology on show is the computer, which, in a room that has so much decorative interest, recedes into relative anonymity rather than dominating.

Aside from choosing antiques as office furnishings, Daniela has also made sure to provide plenty of good-looking storage so she can clear away the day-to-day mess that is inevitably associated with a busy

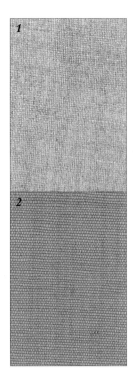

1

2

LEFT The cupboards have been designed to fit neatly around a divan bed which, thanks to its Moroccan-style tufted mattress and bolster cushions at each end, takes on the personality of a sofa when not required as guest accommodation. Fabrics are linens in smoky grays (1) and lilacs (2). Cupboard doors display a gallery of antique maps of Italy protected behind glass, while the sofa alcove encloses and frames a large oil painting.

working life. Two whole walls of this sizeable room are devoted to cupboards and shelves. The bookshelves stacked with reference books and labeled files give the room a quietly academic atmosphere, like that of a library. Full bookshelves are invariably attractive, but Daniela is particularly good at making a pleasing feature of built-in closets, incorporating them in the design of a room so they appear to belong structurally.

All the woodwork in the room is new, including the simple rectangular wall paneling made by applying thin strips of composite board. Above picture-rail level Daniela has used a more complex, fielded panel, which forms a deep frieze around

ANTIQUE MAPS COVER PLAIN DOORS. THESE INTRICATE, MONOCHROME PRINTS TESSELLATE FOR AN EFFECT THAT IS ABSTRACT AND SOPHISTICATED.

ABOVE Small touches like family photographs, a scented candle, and fresh flowers make the room feel personal, comfortable, and lived in. This is not the sort of environment that everyone would find conducive to work, but Daniela takes inspiration from her immediate surroundings and says she would find it impossible to be creative in a space she considered ugly.

the top of the room and continues around the top of the cupboards, drawing them into the overall design so they look integral rather than added on. By leaving a gap between the cupboards, she has created a deep alcove for the sofa and given the room back a few feet of depth. Instead of plain cupboard doors, she has filled their panels with antique maps of Italy, protected behind glass. These intricate, monochrome prints tessellate for an effect that is abstract and sophisticated.

The dominant color in the room is a strong sky blue. All the walls and woodwork are painted in this same flat shade, which is complemented by furnishings in white, cream, and smoky pale mauve. It is a bold choice of color and might be overpowering were it not broken up by the wall of books, the doors of maps, and the large gilt-framed oil painting that hangs above the sofa. As a background and frame for these, the color is a vibrant success.

RIGHT The bed had to be camouflaged so as not to dominate a room also used for work and entertaining. Instead of a sofabed, a desk fits like a sleeve over the end of a plain double divan. The bed is barely noticeable, but the visual space of the alcove can still be enjoyed, and there is no need to unroll bedding every night.

A HARD-WORKING APARTMENT

Discipline and skillful design have shoehorned the essentials of work and home into this small but handsome apartment.

OPPOSITE When work is over, the apartment reverts to its role as a home for Pam and Joseph, and all signs of their busy careers are cleared away. The wooden sliding doors, which hide their collapsible drawing boards, become paneling, a backdrop for the chic white Knoll sofa. The stainless-steel table, used for modelmaking during the day, becomes a dining table.

ABOVE This shelving system holding books, catalogs, and computer equipment is hidden behind a screen of semitranslucent Plexiglas panels set in a wooden frame.
BELOW The few purely decorative pieces in this strictly functional space have high impact. Both the tailor's dummy and the 1970s chrome chandelier have a sculptural presence.

Architect Joseph Marino and interior and product designer Pam Giolito not only live and work together, they also work from home. Nor is their home particularly large. A classic New York studio, built in 1929, their apartment consists of one big room and four very small ones; hall, dressing room, kitchen, and bathroom. This leaves the large room to accommodate working, eating, entertaining, relaxing, and sleeping. A tall order, you would think, for a limited space.

At first glance, this poised and apparently calm interior seems ill equipped to cope with so many functions. Where is the bed, you wonder, and where could anyone, let alone two designers, find the space to spread out their plans and drawings and get on with their work? The answer is twofold. Both Pam and Joseph are disciplined and neat. But discipline and neatness alone would not be enough to make this demanding setup a success. "The key," says Pam, "is not to envisage space in a conventional way, but to borrow space, or rather be flexible with space so areas can adapt to the necessary function."

At night, when the lights are dimmed and the table is laid for dinner, the space takes on the guise of a stylish, modern living room, with its neutral color scheme, its wall of richly grained wood, its generous Knoll sofa, and the quirky decorative details of the tailor's dummy and the 1970s chrome chandelier. But during work hours, the room is transformed into a practical and spacious design studio.

The most surprising part of the transformation is the way the wooden panels slide aside to reveal twin drop-down drafting tables, cork-board walls for

ARCHITECTURE *The layout of the apartment is original except for the alcove, which houses the bed. One wall is paneled with sliding doors, which pull across to hide the two drawing boards.*

LIGHTING *Task lighting for work is also hidden behind the sliding panels. The 1970s chrome chandelier and Gimble ring track lighting are on dimmer switches, so a more intimate atmosphere can be created after hours.*

STORAGE *All the storage has been designed to house specific things. Metal filing cabinets hold business files and household items including the vacuum cleaner. Shelving hidden behind a screen holds books, catalogs, and computer equipment.*

FURNITURE *Wherever possible, furnishings have dual purposes. The stainless-steel table is used as a return for the adjacent drawing board, as a surface for modelmaking, as a focus for meetings, and as a dining table.*

ACCESSORIES *Pam and Joseph collect pottery and limit their buying to "items of great character." They advocate grouping collections "for strength and a more orderly look" while leaving pockets of empty space for a visual rest.*

FLOORING *Floors throughout the apartment are pale wood, except the kitchen, which has white ceramic tiles. A large rectangle of cream carpet marks out the seating area as a place to relax.*

pinning up drawings, special lighting, and drafting equipment, all of which are hidden when not in use. The stainless-steel table from a catering supplier acts as extra desk space for the left-hand drafting table, while the specially made wooden desk, which slides like a sleeve over the end of the bed, serves the same function for the right-hand table. Both these pieces of furniture were chosen to have further uses. The sturdy and easy to clean stainless-steel surface is as practical for modelmaking as it is for serving meals, while the teak desk camouflages the bed so you hardly notice its presence in the room, avoiding the need to screen off the alcove into which it fits so snugly.

ABOVE RIGHT **In a small space every detail counts. Pam and Joseph have eliminated visual clutter to keep the space calm, clean, and functional. The replacement metal windows have been stripped back to the bare aluminum, which makes them look less heavy, and are screened by white wooden Venetian blinds behind white linen curtains. The bar stools serve as seating at the drafting tables as well as at the main table for conference or meals.**
ABOVE LEFT **Opposite the wall of paneling is a wall of good-looking storage. The black filing cabinets provide a surface for the television and stereo, and the chic, asymmetrical shelving above holds magazines.**
BELOW LEFT **The neutral scheme does not compete with client presentations.**

Furnishings have to work hard to earn a place in this multifunctional interior. The neat bar stools (restaurant supply, like the main table) are pulled over to the drafting tables for work, and back around the table for business meetings or meals. Even the purely decorative may be called on. Pam and Joseph collect pottery, some of which they also use for storing tools and anything else small that needs a home.

Crucial for a clutter-free environment is storage, which, according to Pam, must be designed for specific purposes, whether for documents or the vacuum cleaner, and must be easy to access. Pam and Joseph use a combination of filing cabinets, shelves, and cupboards. Some open shelving, which holds computer equipment and other office essentials, is screened behind semitranslucent Plexiglas panels set in wooden frames. Even these hidden shelves are exceptionally neat. But then this is an apartment where everything has its place.

SMART WORK A collaboration between London property developers and an American interior designer created this luxurious, contemporary home office, which combines state-of-the-art technology with the studious, expensive calm of a modern gentlemen's club.

THE DARK POLISHED WOOD AND LEATHER OF THE FURNITURE AND THE GLOSSY STUCCO OF THE WALLS MAKE YOU WANT TO STROKE THEM.

This is interior design at its most swish; a very large apartment in central London, remodeled and fitted out by property developers Tyler London and styled by American interior designer Bill Stubbs. The client is an international businessman, and the flat his equivalent of a sophisticated, luxury hotel suite, but far more personal. In close collaboration, Charles Tyler and Bill Stubbs recently remodeled the apartment to include this study, which leads off the main living room. It was originally a separate room, used as a bedroom, but it had the view of trees, the steady light, and the tranquility to make a perfect home office.

The wall that had divided the bedroom from the living room incorporated the chimney breast. Instead of knocking a door through between the rooms, the wall on each side of the chimney breast came out, and a second fireplace was installed on the study side, back to back with the living room fireplace. The fat pillar of the chimney breast acts as both focus and room divider without detracting from the extra long vistas down each side of the room.

A bank of shelving and drawers and a matching desk are the only furnishings. The effect is sleek and very neat. All the usual detritus of the modern office is notable for its absence; no trailing wires, no black bird's nest of cabling, no loose papers, no stray files. "You would not believe the complexity," says Bill Stubbs, "that underlies this apparent simplicity."

OPPOSITE **The back wall of the room is floor-to-ceiling shelving in glossy Brazilian mahogany, stained almost black. Although this and the desk are part of a line designed specially for offices, with grommets for cabling and storage for files, fax machines, and all the other ugly paraphernalia of business life, they ooze quality, courtesy of finely finished detailing and a lavish use of leather. The shelves are backed with tactile Alcantara in milk-chocolate brown, and** drawers have stiff leather fronts supported on neat metal rods. The attention to detail verges on the obsessive. According to Bill Stubbs, the owner's books looked messy, so he covered them in thick parchment-like paper and specially printed, matching labels. BELOW **Looking into the study past the chimney breast, which now houses a fireplace on both sides.** BELOW LEFT **A row of votive candles on the mantelpiece in glowing amber glass.**

LEFT The shelving includes a ladder, which runs on red wheels supported by a metal track, a witty take on old-fashioned library steps. This attaché case with red stitching attaches to one of the rungs and acts as a pocket for magazines. Leather, with its scent of masculine glamour, is used extensively in a room that is full of sensual texture, from the silky stucco of the walls to the soft folds of the Donghia wool curtains.

The view into the drawing room takes in no fewer than eight pairs of curtains, two for the windows in the study, the rest for the six windows that wrap around the drawing room. A border of polished walnut flooring was left bare so the bottoms of the curtains slide freely when they are electronically opened or closed. The vista was revealed by opening up the walls on each side of the original chimney breast. TOP RIGHT Only the most poised flower arrangement would look at home in this perfectly controlled setting.

Cabling, the undesirable adjunct of modern technology, is ducted beneath the floor. The desk is tailormade to hold a computer and incorporates further ducting and grommets so no more than a few inches of wire need clutter its clean lines. The shelving system is equally accommodating, its leather-fronted drawers fitted out to hold files, fax machines, and other unsightly, if essential, office accessories. Bill Stubbs has even clothed the assorted books on the shelves in matching thick paper covers with specially printed labels. "They just looked too messy," he explains.

Sleek it may be, but to sit in the room is to feel cocooned. Bill Stubbs has introduced warm, if neutral color in the wool curtains, while the dark polished wood and leather of the furniture and the glossy stucco of the walls exude a tactile quality that makes you want to stroke them.

Then there is the lighting. Halogen task lighting is mounted in the ceiling, just behind the desk chair, from where it throws a shadowless, even light. Ambient lighting is provided by the cold cathode lights, which form a cornice of brightness around the edge of the suspended ceiling. The painting above the fireplace has its own light, a directional fiber-optic, with a beam trimmed to fit its dimensions perfectly. And just for fun, and a bit of theater, there are floor-mounted fiber-optic lights, which can be employed to dye the sheer curtains with a wash of different colors.

Like the lighting, the stereo, the gas-effect fires, and the television, the curtains are remote controlled. A border of polished walnut flooring around the edge of the room means that the fabric slides smoothly as they open and shut with an expensive sigh. Or perhaps swish would be a better word.

TRADE SECRETS

RIGHT **Uncompromising color affects our emotions. The red on red on red of this bold room scheme, only mediated through the textures of glossy leather, flat wall paint, and softly shaded velvet, might spell coziness to some, danger to others. The dark portraits look richer and more sober for their all-red setting.**

COLOR

Color is powerful, and because it is powerful, it is also feared. Timid followers of home fashion have largely been spared facing up to this fear for the last ten years or so, thanks to the universal popularity of minimal white. Some of today's most sophisticated designer interiors rely on white and all its bleached and creamy relations. Equally stylish are the schemes that stick to "neutral" colors; browns, taupes, beiges, almost-blacks. In both cases, the look can be subtle and expensive. But it can also be dull and bland.

When it comes to using color more adventurously, it would be easier to be brave if only there were a set of "rules." The color wheel is often quoted as a useful guide. This way of ordering color puts the primary colors at equal distances around a circle and fills the gaps between them with "secondary" colors mixed from them, "tertiary" colors mixed from the secondaries, and so on. The resulting rainbow allows you to pick out the "complementary" colors, which sit opposite one another, and to consider groups of closely related colors. But like all maps, the color wheel can only show one dimension of an immensely complicated world. Add white to any color on the wheel, for example, and you have a "tint"; add black and you have a "shade"; add both and you have a "tone"—all different.

Some decorators have formulated their own rules about color. John Fowler, for example, thought that every room should contain some pink. The truth is that you can follow somebody else's "rules" to the letter, just as you can follow a recipe, but still end up with something you don't like and can't live with. Ask a professional and they will invariably admit to making mistakes with color, even after years of experience and practice. However carefully you choose, however many sample pots you empty, you may still have to try again. There are no easy answers to creating color schemes, but finding the ones that suit you and your interior best is extremely satisfying.

ABOVE **Pale, subtle colors that seem to hover between hues are soothing, like the grayish, greenish, blue of the paint in this bathroom.** LEFT **Mary Shaw favors warmer colors, but her use of tweed, incorporating flecks of many shades, means strong colors such as orange are never harsh.**

RIGHT Designer Voon Wong uses planes of different color to differentiate areas of his open-plan apartment. The orange strip running along the front of the built-in bench in the dining area jumps forward in sharp contrast to the shadowy blue of the wall behind.

ABOVE This hall uses blocks of pastel blue and pink and a pale orange for an effect that is far from babyish.
RIGHT White and off-white accessorized with touches of black invariably look sophisticated.
BELOW Fresh and pretty blue and white must be one of the most enduringly popular color schemes.

INSPIRATION can be found anywhere and everywhere. Look at your wardrobe. Look in your garden. Tear pictures out of magazines, take samples of fabric, and make a collage of the colors you like together.

LIGHT AND COLOR interrelate in a complex and fascinating way. The same color can look quite different in natural and artificial lights, in the morning and in the evening, and on different walls of the same room.

PALE COLORS reflect light and make rooms look larger and brighter, while dark colors absorb it, drawing walls in for a cozy and enclosed feel.

TEXTURE also affects color and how it is perceived. When designing a color scheme with a limited palette, remember that differences in texture add interest and depth.

TEST paint colors on large pieces of board that you can carry around a room and try propped on different walls. Painting the inside of a cardboard box will show you how a color varies in light and shade.

RULES are there to be broken. Never be too frightened, or lazy, to experiment—it will be worth it in the end.

RIGHT AND FAR RIGHT
**Two traditional kitchen
floorings with very different
effects. Pale limestone,
machined to perfect
smoothness and laid in
large tiles, looks modern
and expensive, while the
checkerboard of black and
white ceramic tiles is stylish
with an old-fashioned feel.**

FLOORING

The floor is the foundation for any room scheme and
has a profound effect on its atmosphere, as well as
appearance. The floor is also the most used and
abused surface in any house; battered by feet, scraped
by furniture, and requiring regular vacuuming,
brushing, mopping, or sweeping.

Different parts of a house make different demands
on their respective floor coverings. Some, like halls,
stairs, corridors, and routes between well-used areas,
require a floor that is particularly hard-wearing.
Bathrooms, especially those with showers, work better
if the flooring is waterproof. Kitchens work better if
the flooring is stain-resistant. Bedrooms feel more
comfortable if at least some of the floor is soft and
warm to the touch of a bare foot.

As no single material can comply perfectly with all
these domestic demands, the tendency is to choose
room-specific flooring. This is all very sensible, but
can result in an interior that feels fragmented and
jumpy as you step from quarry tiles in the hall to
stripped floorboards in the living room to linoleum
in the kitchen to carpet on the stairs, and so on.

Using a single type of flooring that flows from room
to room is one of the tricks designers use to make a
space appear larger; walls seem to "float" as if the
floor slipped beneath them, and the eye follows the
floor through doorways, along corridors, and across
landings in seamless vistas. Probably the most practical
choices of single flooring are some kind of stone tile
(pale limestone is particularly fashionable), or wood.

Both wood and stone can be softened with the
addition of rugs, to mark out seating areas in living
rooms, or create islands of warmth in bedrooms. For
bathrooms and kitchens, both wood and stone can be
sealed to be stain- and water-resistant. Wall-to-wall
carpet may be appropriate for upstairs bedrooms,
where it muffles sound and makes rooms feel
luxuriously cozy. Some people like carpet in
bathrooms as well, but if you prefer a washable
surface, using tiles that are close in color to the carpet
helps to maintain the visual unity between rooms.

ABOVE **If you are fortunate
enough to have an original
floor as beautiful as this
inlaid marquetry, you would
be foolish to cover it with
carpet. Reclaimed antique
flooring is an alternative to
using new wood and can be
an excellent investment.**
LEFT **A sleek metal shower
tray teams contemporary
efficiency and hygiene.**

RIGHT Carpet is still the softest, warmest, and most forgiving of floor coverings. It can be inconspicuous, laid wall to wall in a disappearing shade of pale mushroom, or it can be a potent presence, like this strawberry-red rug with its pattern of raised tufting. The thicker its pile, the more you feel tempted to sit on the floor.

RIGHT AND BELOW The combination of wooden floors overlaid with natural matting provides a base of neutral color and works equally well in a period house as in a loft conversion. There are many gentle variations of color and differences in texture to choose between, and squares of matting can be bound at the edges with cotton, linen, or leather.

SPEND as much as you can afford. Flooring is disruptive and expensive to change. A floor that looks and feels beautiful, and sounds solid underfoot, is an excellent interior investment.

ACOUSTICS have a subtle but pervasive influence over the atmosphere of any indoor space. Large areas of unrelieved hard flooring, such as stone or tiles, make for harsh acoustics unless dampened by soft furnishings. Wood is more gentle, although wooden stairs and sprung wooden floors tend to clatter and reverberate underfoot. Again, runners and rugs will mute the effect.

CONSIDER COLOR. Pale flooring reflects more light into a dark room. A dark floor, on the other hand, can "ground" a room that is light enough already. A very shiny dark floor acts like a mirror and increases the impression of height in a room.

NATURAL floorings, whether wood, stone, or vegetable mattings, are more likely to wear and weather gracefully than synthetics. Their gentle, earthy colors seem appropriate underfoot, just as the pale blues, grays, and off-whites of the sky seem right for ceilings.

A SQUARE or rectangle of carpet or matting, bound at the edges, can unify a room with odd corners and angles.

PLAIN MATS can also be used in larger spaces to divide the room into "zones," whether for dining or relaxing in a sociable group.

RIGHT AND FAR RIGHT **Old-fashioned wall lights like these, with glass shades and brass fixtures, were originally designed for gas and are appropriate for rooms with a period feel. Original antique light fixtures can be converted to electricity, but reproductions offer a greater choice and are less expensive.**

BELOW **Sleek modern interiors demand sleek modern lighting, and the choice has never been more extensive. Here a strip light casts a warm glow over the open-plan dining area, a far cry from the nasty, flickering tubes that used to be the bane of so many offices, while the cleaner, brighter light of halogen bulbs is used in the kitchen.**

LIGHTING

The loveliest room can be disfigured after dark by a single light bulb. One bright overhead light strips charm, distorts color, and erases texture. The converse is also true. A room that is plain ugly by day can be transformed at night in the glow of a few well-placed candles.

Generally speaking, the more natural daylight in a room the better; while houses should provide shelter from intense heat and blinding sunshine, rooms that are bright enough not to require added artificial lighting by day are rooms that feel good to live in.

At night, however, we are reliant on artificial light. Aside from the old-fashioned candle, which is more popular than ever as a decorative feature and mood-enhancer, there are three main types of light source available for the modern home: the tungsten bulb, which produces a light with a creamy yellow cast; the halogen bulb, which emits a crisp, white light; and the fluorescent tube, which has improved beyond measure since the days when its flickering white rods cast a nasty bluish hue.

If you are building from scratch or have a large budget for lighting alone, you can turn your house into a theater of light with several separate circuits in each room, and a range of settings from bright and cheery to low and moody, controlled at the press of a button. However, as long as you provide several different light sources, it is perfectly possible to create a lighting scheme that is both adaptable and attractive, without being particularly expensive.

Different activities make different demands on lighting. Bathrooms, for example, should have lights on each side of any mirror used for shaving or make-up, while kitchens need strong overhead lighting directed onto work surfaces, sinks, and stoves. A bedroom should have a light for reading and a stronger light for dressing. Beyond these basics you can play with light and its effects, even if the game is as simple as moving a gooseneck around.

LEFT **These wall lights are more decorative than functional, but they cast an exceptionally pretty glow as the candle flame is reflected in the mosaic of mirror.** RIGHT **A more up-to-date means of creating atmosphere with light is provided by these floor-mounted uplighters, which cast oval rings of brightness onto the white Roman shades when they are lowered at night.**

RIGHT **Proportion** is as important a consideration in lighting as in any other aspect of furnishing. The size and level of this large lantern, which hangs low into the stairwell, seem right for such a grand hall.
FAR RIGHT **Placing tall table lamps in pairs gives formal bones for an arrangement on a tabletop.**

CONTROL. Some designers insist that dimmer switches are a minimum requirement. If you can only install them in two rooms, choose the living room and the dining area, even if the latter is part of the former.

A CENTRAL PENDANT LIGHT can make a grand decorative gesture, whether a glorious glass chandelier or the globe of a wire and paper shade. In both cases, the bigger, the better. Just don't be tempted to turn it on— a strong overhead light is not flattering.

WALL LIGHTS give an attractive wash of light at a lower and more complimentary level than ceiling lights, but beware of their placing. Because they are fixed, it is not a good idea to position them on either side of a piece of furniture that you might want to move or change, for example.

LARGE rooms need more light sources than smaller ones. It may be worth installing floor-recessed sockets in strategic positions to avoid the nuisance, and danger, of trailing flexes.

RECESSED ceiling lights with small, bright halogen bulbs are ideal for any room with a low ceiling.

FIBER-OPTIC lights are ideal for bathrooms because the light source can be placed outside the room and protected from getting wet.

RIGHT **Fabrics that seem to coordinate by accident create a relaxed feel in any room. Here, the room is a kitchen, with space for a sofa and generous curtains. The red and white check tablecloth picks up the red flowers of the chintz, while the muted stripe on the sofa matches the greenish grays of the foliage.**

FABRICS

Fabrics are as essential to comfort as water is to cleanliness. A room with no fabrics may look terribly chic, but feels strangely unwelcoming. The most super-efficient stainless-steel kitchen gains a certain humanity from its neatly hung linen dishtowels.

The current fashion is for fabrics that are plain, simple, and even humble. After the gorgeous excesses of the 1980s, when no suburban window was complete without its full complement of swags, drapes, tiebacks, and tassels, our collective taste has quietened down and our appetite for endless pattern and fancy trimmings subsided.

As interest in pattern has faded to a muted choice of gentle chintzes, simple stripes and checks, and sophisticated monochrome toiles, texture has become more important. Leather covers chairs, floors, and shelving; suede covers cushions; ponyskin, cowskin, and sheepskin make rugs; and all manner of strokeable fake fur drapes over beds and sofas. In room schemes that use predominantly solid fabrics, visual and tactile interest comes from the contrasts in finish and feel: glossy brown leather with downy brown velvet; rough linen trimmed with gleaming satin; hairy tweed with silky cashmere.

There has also been a willingness to experiment and use fabrics "incorrectly." Gauze, designed for culinary purposes, makes clear curtains and hangings that are as cheap as they are romantic. Cream muslin, once the underwear of upholstery, is now widely used for upholstery and slipcovers. Heavy artist's canvas makes curtains that fall in fat folds. Antique sheets in coarse linen make fresh and charmingly crumpled slipcovers. All the rules of decorating decorum have been broken as tweeds stretch over armchairs and saris waft at windows.

This makes decorating with fabrics all the more fun. You don't need to spend hours poring over swatches, you can raid street markets and thrift stores, use dress fabrics and antique fabrics. However, like all things worth doing, putting together a scheme using different fabrics, however relaxed and spontaneous the result may look, is difficult. Trial, error, and blatant plagiarism can all play their part.

ABOVE **Dressing a chair can radically alter its character. Here a tight sheath of white cotton, split to the thigh, emphasizes curves.**
LEFT **A gathered curtain makes inexpensive hidden storage. Here, a washed-out mauve gingham is matched by a mosaic-tiled backsplash in a similar color.**

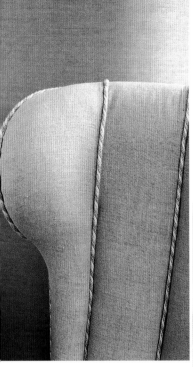

RIGHT Many companies make "document" fabrics, copied from antique ones. These delicately patterned curtains are an eighteenth-century design and add pretty, period glamour to an Edwardian window.
BELOW A looser, informal pattern of dog roses printed on linen has a more timeless appeal, here used as a runner.

ABOVE Fitted upholstery is formal dress for furniture, here made even smarter and crisper by the addition of contrasting piping, which follows and emphasizes the unusual shaped back of a wing chair.
BELOW Voile and velvet on a voluptuous little sofa create a look that is feminine and indulgent.

CHEAP FABRICS like cotton duck make excellent curtains, but don't skimp on quantity or the quality of making. Similarly, dress a chair or sofa upholstered in plain muslin with pillows in sumptuous fabrics. Both are ways of saving money while achieving an expensive-looking effect.

THROWS are a simple and fashionable means to add color and texture that can be changed at whim. Swap a fake fur and velvet throw draped over the back of the sofa for a dove-gray feather-light pashmina blanket and you have left winter behind.

CONSIDER changing curtains from heavy to light and adding cotton slipcovers to chairs and sofas to give a room a summer facelift.

SMALL windows that admit insufficient light will be smothered by curtains unless they draw well away from the embrasure. Valances also cut out light. Slim shades take up minimal space and admit maximum light when open.

CUSHIONS should be bigger than you think. Undersized pillows look cheap.

HANGINGS. If you fall in love with a fabric that is beyond your budget for curtains, consider buying a length to use as a wall hanging and having plain curtains instead.

RIGHT **Painted wooden furniture has a quality of humble elegance that refers back to the seventeenth and eighteenth centuries, when only inferior quality wood such as pine was disguised by added color. This kitchen puts copies of Swedish Gustavian chairs with a Victorian pine table, the legs of which have been painted to match them.**

FURNITURE

There are some basic pieces of furniture we would all be loath to live without; a comfortable bed, a sturdy table, a supportive chair, a squashy sofa, cupboards and drawers for hanging clothes and hiding clutter, shelves for books. Your choice will be determined by taste and budget, as well as practicality.

In addition to these basics, you may also own furniture that has been handed down from parents or inherited. You may have adopted things when you moved in with a partner and pooled resources. And you are highly likely to have at least one piece of furniture that is neither useful nor practical but that you love nonetheless.

Sometimes professional decorators start with an empty room, but more usually, when working for private clients, they are obliged to incorporate furnishings that a client refuses to sacrifice at the altar of pure design. Comfortable homes, as opposed to show homes or hotel rooms, almost always embrace compromise. Furniture that doesn't initially appeal can often be disguised; headboards can be changed, sofas recovered, chairs painted or stripped, cushions added or taken away. An unattractive table can be hidden under a long tablecloth, a dreary cupboard can be brought up to date with new handles.

Before you rush out and buy new things, always look at what you already have and what can be done with it. Move things round. Try a sofa you don't like in a bedroom (test the space with a template first to save your back), or a kitchen table as a desk, or a desk as a dressing table. Furniture can be surprisingly adaptable and look quite different in another room and put to another use. And don't always imagine it will be cheaper to buy new. Sometimes an antique can be less expensive as well as a better investment.

ABOVE **This bed takes center stage, thanks to its Shaker-inspired design. Its elongated posts reach to the ceiling as if it were trying to grow into a four-poster.**
LEFT **Soft furnishings, like this daybed with rounded edges and padded pillows, can seem to be beckoning you for an afternoon nap.**

Storage is essential to physical and mental neatness and calm. Sadly, the rule is that you can never have enough, as somehow the space available will always be full. Built-in furniture (LEFT) is often the best way to maximize shelf and hanging space and, carefully designed, it can be stylish and attractive. The advantage of freestanding cupboards and shelves (RIGHT) is that you can take them with you or move them around.

RIGHT A living room without a sofa is like a bedroom without a bed. Big squashy sofas like these, with relaxed slipcovers, are particularly irresistible. The fact that they don't match adds to the informality. BELOW An antique, like this beautifully turned chair, often has the added charm of the genuinely handmade.

SIZE does matter. All rooms need at least one large piece of furniture so as not to look bitty.

NEVER be afraid to mix the old with the new. Although it may feel safer to stick with one style or period, whether twenty-first-century Conran or eighteenth-century mahogany, juxtapositions and contrasts are much more stylish and provide real visual excitement.

BUILT-IN and customized storage may be more expensive than its off-the-shelf equivalent, but you will get much more cupboard and shelf space for your money and the effect will be more streamlined.

COMFORT is more important than style when it comes to choosing beds, dining chairs, office chairs, and sofas. Always lie or sit on them for as long as you can get away with before buying.

PLANNING. When trying to decide where large pieces of furniture will fit in a room, make a plan to scale with graph paper and try out different arrangements with templates. You can also use full-size paper templates in the room itself.

GUILT. Don't let guilt about unwanted wedding presents or hideous inheritances spoil a room. If the piece you don't like can't be disguised or tucked out of sight in a spare room, either put it in the attic or sell it.

RIGHT **Books furnish a room; they make it look lived in and are a magnet for most first-time visitors, revealing the interests and tastes of their owner from a quick scan of their spines.**

FINISHING TOUCHES

There are so many finishing touches that transform a house into a home it is difficult to know where to start. Most, however, fall into two main categories; pictures and ornaments. These are some of the most personal items in any house, the accessories that make a room complete and that betray much more about the taste, history, and even the character of its owner than the curtains, sofa, or color scheme.

Most of us have succumbed to the zeitgeist of the last decade and pared down our interiors. Clutter, however cheery and intimate, is definitively out of vogue. Less continues to be more, and the smartest rooms are enlivened by strictly edited displays of anything purely decorative.

This does not mean that all treasured collections, whether of china or hats, must be consigned to the attic, or that your array of family photographs has to remain firmly inside the pages of an album. But if you don't want your house to look unfashionably full, it does mean that care must be taken about grouping things while leaving empty spaces between for the room to breathe. Wall-to-wall clutter is not only unfashionable, it is claustrophobic.

Grouping and color matching are both key for taming an excess of objects. A hutch loaded with a display of all-white china, or a wall of photographs identically framed, create a more graphic look than if the china were in a rainbow of colors and the photographs on top of the piano and every occasional table. Very small things, whether snuff boxes or cufflinks, tend to look better behind glass, corraled in a cabinet or display case. Mixed groupings—those studied still lifes that designers call "tablescapes"—can be stunning, but require an educated eye. Looking at an arrangement through a camera or just framed by your fingers can help you to see what works.

Picture hanging is similarly demanding but even more important unless you are a confirmed minimalist. Positioning is crucial; too high, too low, too far to one side, too crowded, too lonely, all look dreadful. Dotting pictures evenly around a room is just as bad. Far better, if your pictures are on the small side, to gather them together. Alternatively, a single large picture can look very dramatic.

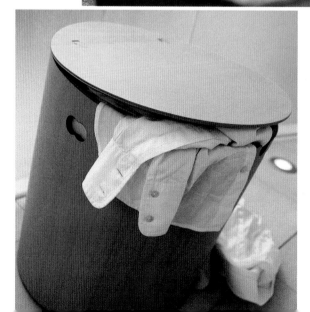

ABOVE **Pillows add comfort and character to a plain chair or sofa, while offering the opportunity to play with color, texture, pattern, and trimmings on a relatively small scale.** LEFT **Even the humble laundry basket can be a thing of beauty. This is one of which William Morris would surely approve.**

LEFT AND RIGHT
Deliberate asymmetry is a visual challenge. In this plain bathroom the only accessory is the mirror, but the angle of the tub gives a quirky charm. Grouping pictures without the safety net of symmetry is an art. The mix of pictures and chairs succeeds because of the attention to balance, and the frame made by the doors.

RIGHT You can't beat fresh flowers for bringing life to any room. If they have scent, it is an added bonus.
BELOW This is a collection with humor as well as charm; a gathering of antique toys on wheels, simply mounted and grouped to look as though they are trying to run away.

BOOKS not only decorate a room, they supply another dimension of interest and stimulus. Some decorators go to immense lengths to make books look neat, arranging them strictly by size and color, or even dressing them in new, uniform dust jackets.

SYMMETRY or straight rows of the same thing are two ways of ordering objects that the eye invariably finds pleasing.

MIRROR is one of the professional decorator's most useful and versatile tools. Wherever it goes, it conjures space and light, whether used to enclose a tub, top a table, or line a wall.

HANGING PICTURES is an art. When planning a group, start with the middle picture, which should be hung at about eye level. Design the layout by laying them on the floor first. You can also cut out templates and mount them temporarily on the wall.

SMELL is incredibly important. A bad smell makes an interior feel repugnant. But the scents of fresh flowers, beeswax polish, warm bread, or a really good-quality scented candle are irresistible and relaxing.

IF YOU SEE SOMETHING YOU LOVE, buy it and then find a place for it.

RESOURCES

FURNITURE AND ACCESSORIES

ABC Carpet & Home
888 Broadway
New York, NY 10003
212 473 3000
Visit www.abchome.com for
a retail outlet near you.
*An eclectic collection of furnishings,
linens, rugs, and other home accessories.*

Alabaster
597 Hayes Street
San Francisco, CA 94102
415 558 0482
www.alabastersf.com
Unique collectibles and home accessories.

**The Annex Antique Fair
and Flea Market**
West 39th Street
New York, NY
212 243 5343
www.hellskitchenfleamarket.com
*Manhattan's primary flea market takes
place every Saturday and Sunday,
year-round.*

Anthropologie
Rittenhouse Square
1801 Walnut Street
Philadelphia, PA 19103
215 568 2114
Visit the website to find a store
near you.
www.anthropologie.com.
*Vintage-inspired one-of-a-kind home
accessories, furniture, hardware, rugs,
and drapes.*

Bobbie King Antiques
667 Duling Avenue
Jackson, MS 39216
601 362 9803
*Antique and contemporary collectibles
and furnishing.*

The Bombay Company, Inc.
P.O. Box 161009
Fort Worth, TX 76161
Call 800 956 1782 or visit
www.bombaycompany.com to
find a store near you.
*Reproductions of classic, often British
colonial-style furnishings and accessories.*

Bremermann Designs
3943 Magazine Street
New Orleans, LA 70015
504 891 7763
www.bremermanndesigns.com
French antiques and accessories.

Brimfield Antique Show
Route 20
Brimfield, MA 01010
www.brimfieldshow.com
*This famous flea market runs for a
week in May, July, and September.*

Chequers of Aspen
520 East Cooper
Aspen, CO 81611
970 925 7572
www.chequersofaspen.com
*Quality contemporary and antique
home furnishings.*

The Conran Shop
407 East 59th Street
New York, NY 10022
866 755 9079
www.conranusa.com
Cutting-edge design.

Country Farm Furniture
148 Front Street
Bath, ME 04530
207 443 2367
www.qualityfurniture.com
*Finely designed and crafted country-
style furniture.*

Crate & Barrel
646 N. Michigan Avenue
Chicago, IL 60611
800 967 6696
Visit www.crateandbarrel.com for
a retail outlet near you.
*A big source of good-value furniture
and accessories, from white china and
glass to dining-room sets and beds.*

English Country Antiques
26 Snake Hollow Road
Bridgehampton, NY 11932
613 537 0606
www.ecantiques.com
Period country furniture and accessories.

Englishtown Auction Sales
90 Wilson Avenue
Englishtown, NJ 07726
732 446 9644
www.englishtownauction.com
*This 100-acre market attracts
professional and amateur dealers. Open
Saturday and Sunday, year-round.*

Ethan Allen
Ethan Allen Drive
P.O. Box 1966
Danbury, CT 06813
Call 888 EAHELP1 or visit
www.ethanallen.com for a retail
outlet near you.
Fine furniture for every room.

www.fleamarket.com
Visit this website for details of flea
markets around the country.

Form + Function
3232 South Highland Drive
Salt Lake City, UT 84106
801 467 3131
www.formfunction.net
*Specializes in modern furniture and
accessories for the home.*

Georgetown Flea Market
Arlington County Court House
Washington, D.C.
202 775 FLEA
www.georgetownfleamarket.com
*If you visit the nation's capital, this is
a stop worth making. Open Sundays,
March through December.*

Gump's
135 Post Street
San Francisco, CA 94108
800 882 8055
www.gumps.com
*Luxury home furnishings for every
room of the house.*

Herman Miller Inc.
855 East Main Avenue
Zeeland, MI 49464-0302
888 443 4357
www.hermanmiller.com
*Official U.S. importer of Artek
furniture, including Alvar Aalto
and other fine twentieth-century
furniture designers.*

Highbrow Inc.
2110 8th Avenue South
Nashville, TN 37204
888 329 0219
www.highbrowfurniture.com
*Dealer of vintage modern furniture,
textiles, and lighting.*

Howard Kaplan Designs
240 East 60th Street
New York, NY 10022
646 443 7170
www.howardkaplandesigns.com
*Specializes in 19th- and 18th-century
French and English antiques, as well
as fine reproductions.*

IKEA
1800 East McConnor Parkway
Schaumburg, IL 60173
Call 800 434 IKEA or visit
www.ikea.com for a store
near you.
*Simple but well-designed furniture
you have to assemble yourself, plus
inexpensive storage and kitchenware.*

Jennifer Convertibles
1634 Wisconsin Avenue NW
Washington, D.C. 20001
202 342 5496
Visit www.jenniferfurniture.com
for the store nearest to you.
*Stylish sleeper sofas, armchairs,
and rugs.*

Jensen-Lewis
89 Seventh Avenue
New York, NY 10011
212 929 4880
www.jensen-lewis.com
*A full selection of modern home
furnishings and housewares.*

Maine Cottage
Lower Falls Landing
106 Lafayette Street
Yarmouth, ME 04096
207 846 3699
Visit www.mainecottage.com to
find a dealer near you.
*Simple, hardworking furniture for every
room of the house.*

Moderne Gallery
111 North Third Street
Philadelphia, PA 19106
215 923 8536
www.modernegallery.com
Twentieth-century furnishings.

Moss
150 Greene Street
New York, NY 10012
866 888 6677
www.mossonline.com
*Contemporary accessories
and furniture.*

NOVICA
11835 West Olympic Boulevard,
Suite 750E
Los Angeles, CA 90064
877 2 NOVICA
www.novica.com
*This online store has teamed up with
National Geographic to provide
unique home furnishings and art
directly from artisans working
around the world.*

Picc-a-dilly Flea Market
796 West 13th Street (Lane County
Fairgrounds)
Eugene, OR
541 683 5589
*Dealers from all over sell a wide
variety of antiques and collectibles here
every Sunday, except July and August.*

Pier One Imports
71 Fifth Avenue
New York, NY 10003
Call 212 206 1911 or visit
www.pier1.com to find a store
near you.
*Affordable home accessories and
furniture from all over the world.*

Pottery Barn
600 Broadway
New York, NY 10012
212 219 2420
www.potterybarn.com
Quality furniture and home accessories.

R 20th Century Design
82 Franklin Street
New York, NY 10013
212 343 7979
www.r20thcentury.com
*A comprehensive selection of mid-
century modern furniture, lighting, and
accessories from the most important
designers and manufacturers.*

Restoration Hardware
935 Broadway
New York, NY 10010
212 260 9479
www.restorationhardware.com
*Fine hardware, including flooring,
curtains, and lighting, but also
furniture and accessories for the home.*

Room Service Vintage
107 East North Loop
Austin, TX 78751
512 451 1057
www.roomservicevintage.com
*This vintage and collectibles store also
has a warehouse selling larger pieces.*

Rose Bowl Flea Market
100 Rose Bowl Drive
Pasadena, CA
323 560 7469
www.rgcshows.com
*This famous fleamarket on the second
Sunday of every month has everything
from retro kitsch to fine furnishings.*

Ruby Beets Antiques
25 Washington Street
P.O. Box 1174
Sag Harbor, NY 11963
631 899 3275
www.rubybeets.com
Painted furniture, vintage kitchenware.

Sage Street Antiques
Sage Street (off Route 114)
Sag Harbor, NY 11963
631 725 4036
Period furniture and accessories.

Scavenger Hunt
3438 Clairmont Road NE
Atlanta, GA 30319
404 634 4948
Vintage items for the home.

Shaker Style
292 Chesham Road
Harrisville, NH 03450
888 824 3340
www.shakerstyle.com
Custom-built Shaker-style furniture.

**Swartzendruber Hardwood
Creations**
1100 Chicago Avenue
Goshen, IN 46528
800 531 2502
www.swartzendruber.com
*French-country, Shaker, and Prairie-
style quality reproductions.*

Takashimaya
693 Fifth Avenue
New York, NY 10022
212 350 0100
*This Japanese department store
features exclusive bed linens,
scented candles, and other
luxurious tabletop accessories.*

Pueblo of Tesuque Flea Market
North of Highway 85, on the
Santa Fe Opera Grounds
Santa Fe, NM
505 955 7767
www.tesuquepueblofleamarket.com
*This market specializes in
Southwestern antiques and
collectibles and is held Fridays,
Saturdays, and Sundays throughout
spring, summer, and fall.*

20CDesign.com
214 821 0262
www.20cdesign.com
*Specializes in Italian and
Scandinavian modern designs.*

Uncommon Objects
1512 South Congress Avenue
Austin, TX 78704
512 442 4000
The name says it all.

Unica Home
7540 Dean Martin Drive, Suite 501
Las Vegas, NV 89139-5965
888 89 UNICA
www.unicahome.com
*A wide range of modern furniture
and accessories, both vintage and
reproductions, from top designers.*

Up the Creek Antiques
American Antique Furniture
Market
209 North Tower
Centralia, WA 98531
360 330 0427
www.amerantfurn.com
*Antique furniture and lighting, from
Victorian to Arts and Crafts, restored
or in its original condition.*

Water Street Antiques
78 Main Street
Sutter Creek, CA 95685
209 267 0585
www.waterstreetantiques.com
Fine antiques.

Williamsburg Marketplace
800 414 6291
www.williamsburgmarketplace.com
*Historically accurate reproductions of
Colonial pewter, prints, and other
decorative accessories.*

Workbench
470 Park Avenue South
New York, NY 10016
212 481 5454
*Clean and functional modern furniture
for bedrooms, dining, and living rooms,
storage, and more.*

KITCHENS AND
TABLEWARE

Bosch
5551 McFadden Avenue
Huntington Beach, CA 92649
800 944 2904
www.boschappliances.com
Kitchen appliances and fixtures.

RESOURCES

Bulthaup
578 Broadway, Suite 306
New York, NY 10012
212 966 7183
800 808 2923 for other stockists
www.bulthaup.com
Contemporary and high-tech kitchens, high quality and clever design.

Fishs Eddy
869 Broadway
New York, NY 10003
212 420 2090
www.fishseddy.com
Overstock supplies of simple mugs, plates, bowls, and other tableware.

Fortunoff
681 Fifth Avenue
New York, NY 10022
212 758 6660
www.fortunoff.com
Fine antique and estate silver and other giftware for the home.

Kohler Co.
Call 800 456 4537 or visit www.kohlerco.com for dealers.
Modern kitchen furniture, plumbing, and sinks.

Michael Fina
545 Fifth Avenue
New York, NY 10017
800 BUY FINA
www.michaelcfina.com
Exclusive tableware, including silver, glass, and china.

Poggenpohl
350 Passaic Avenue
Fairfield, NJ 07004
973 812 8900
www.poggenpohl-usa.com
Specializes in custom kitchen designs.

Tabletools
310 601 7612
www.tabletools.com
Online retailer of well-designed kitchen and tableware.

William Yeoward
www.williamyeowardcrystal.com
Beautiful contemporary crystal from this talented designer. Stocked nationwide, including Neiman Marcus, Bergdorf Goodman, and Saks Fifth Avenue.

Williams-Sonoma
121 East 59th Street
New York, NY 10022
917 369 1131
Visit www.williams-sonomainc.com for a retail outlet near you.
Specializes in utensils and tableware for gourmets and everyday cooks.

BED AND BATH ACCESSORIES

Barneys New York
660 Madison Avenue
New York, NY 10021
212 826 8900
www.barneys.com
Fine linens and accessories.

Bed Bath & Beyond
620 Sixth Avenue
New York, NY 10011
212 255 3550
Call 800 462 3966 or visit the website for a store near you.
www.bedbathandbeyond.com
Everything for the bedroom and bathroom, plus kitchen utensils and storage solutions.

Bedside Manor
6822-E Phillips Place Court
Charlotte, NC 28210
866 554 7727
www.bedsidemanor.com

Bella Linea Nashville
West Gate Center
6031 Highway 100
Nashville, TN 37205
615 352 4041
Exquisite linens, down, and bath items.

Clawfoot Supply
at Signature Hardware
2700 Crescent Springs Pike
Erlanger, KY 41017
877 682 4192
www.clawfootsupply.com
Complete supply of authentic reproduction clawfoot tubs, pedestal and console sinks, Topaz copper soaking tubs, and more.

The Company Store
500 Company Store Road
La Crosse, WI 54601
800 323 8000
www.thecompanystore.com
Online retailer of accessories for bedroom and bath.

Gabberts Inc.
3501 Galleria
Edina, MN 55435
952 927 1500
www.gabberts.com
Quality linens.

Garnet Hill
231 Main Street
Franconia, NH 03580
800 870 3513
www.garnethill.com
An online retailer of natural-fiber duvets, pillows, and linens.

Gracious Home
1220 Third Avenue
New York, NY 10021
212 517 6300
www.gracioushome.com
Bedding, linens, and fine fixtures.

Levine Linens
Phoenix, AZ
602 944 2898
Linens and other bedroom accessories, available through your decorator.

Portico Bed & Bath
72 Spring Street
New York, NY 10012
212 941 7800
Fine linens and luxury beds.

Ralph Lauren Home Collection
379 West Broadway
New York, NY 10012
212 625 1660
www.rlhome.polo.com
Home accessories including linens, tableware, and towels.

Wamsutta
Springs Global Inc.
P.O. Box 70
Fort Mill, SC 29716
Call 888 926 7888 for outlets.
www.springs.com
A wide range of linens, including flannels and duvet covers.

Waterworks
23 West Putnam Avenue
Greenwich, CT 06830
800 899 6757 for other stockists.
www.waterworks.com
Bathroom fixtures, furniture, and lights.

WORK ROOMS

California Closets
800 274 6754
www.californiaclosets.com
Customized storage solutions, not just for home offices but every room.

Pressman Design Studio
451 Miller Road
East Greenbush, NY 12061
518 479 0012
www.pressmandesign.com
Home office and storage solutions.

PAINTS

Benjamin Moore Paints
101 Paragon Drive
Montvale, NJ 07645
Visit the website for stockists.
www.benjaminmoore.com
Fine paints.

Farrow & Ball
D&D Building, Suite 1519
979 Third Avenue
New York NY 10022
212 752 5544
www.farrow-ball.com
Unbeatable for subtle paint colors with strange names, including the National Trust ranges, also papers and varnishes.

Janovic
1150 Third Avenue
New York, NY 10021
212 772 1400
www.janovic.com
Quality paints in a wide color range.

**The Old Fashioned Milk
Paint Co.**
436 Main Street
P.O. Box 222
Groton, MA 01450
978 448 6336
www.milkpaint.com
*These paints replicate the color and
finish of Colonial and Shaker antiques.*

Pittsburgh Paints
One PPG Place
Pittsburg, PA 15272
888 774 1010
www.ppg.com

**Pratt and Lambert
Historic Paints**
www.prattandlambert.com
*150-year-old producer of top
of the line paints.*

Sherwin Williams
Check the website to find
a retailer near you.
www.sherwin-williams.com

FLOORING

Anderson Hardwood Flooring
P.O. Box 1155
Clinton, SC 29325
864 833 6250
www.andersonfloors.com
Large selection of hardwood flooring.

Authentic Pine Floors, Inc.
4042 Highway 42
Locust Grove, GA 30248
770 957 6038
Wide plank and heart pine flooring.

A Candle in the Night
181 Main Street
Brattleboro, VT 05301
802 257 0471
www.acandleinthenight.com
Quality Persian and Turkish rugs.

Country Floors
15 East 16th Street
New York, NY 10003
212 627 8300
www.countryfloors.com
*American and imported ceramics
and terra-cotta.*

Linoleum City
5657 Santa Monica Boulevard
Hollywood, CA 90038
323 469 0063
www.linoleumcity.com
*Every kind of linoleum, from period
to modern to high-tech.*

Native Tiles and Ceramics
2317 Border Avenue
Torrance, CA 90501
310 533 8684
www.nativetile.com
Reproduction tiles.

Paris Ceramics
150 East 58th Street, 7th Floor
New York, NY 10155
212 644 2782
www.parisceramics.com
*Limestone, terra-cotta, antique stone,
and hand-painted tiles.*

River City Woodworks
1305 Wisteria Drive
Metairie, LA 70005
504 899 7278
*Antique pine flooring, moldings,
doors, and stair parts.*

LIGHTING

Boyd Lighting
944 Folsom Street
San Francisco, CA 94107
415 778 4300
www.boydlighting.com

Brass Light Gallery
131 South First Street
Milwaukee, WI 53204
800 243 9595
www.brasslight.com

Flos Inc.
200 McKay Road
Huntington Station, NY 11746
631 549 2745
www.flos.com

Hafele America Co.
3901 Cheyenne Drive
Archdale, NC 27263
800 423 3531
www.hafele.com/us

Knoll
800 343 5665
www.knoll.com
*Selection of modern and ergonomic
desk lamps from original designers.*

Lighting Collaborative
333 Park Avenue South, Suite B
New York, NY 10010
212 253 7220
www.lightingcollaborative.com
Electro Track lighting supplier.

Philips Lighting
200 Franklin Square Drive
Somerset, NJ 08873
732 563 1130
www.lighting.philips.com

FABRIC AND WINDOW TREATMENTS

Berwick Offray
800 BERWICK
www.offray.com
*Fabric, notions, and trims from
retailers nationwide.*

Calico Corners
203 Gale Lane
Kennett Square, PA 19348
800 213 6366
www.calicocorners.com
Vast range of furnishing fabrics.

Clarence House Fabrics, Ltd.
979 Third Avenue, Suite 205
New York, NY 10022
800 211 4704
www.clarencehouse.com
*Natural-fiber fabrics with prints based
on 15th- to 20th-century documents.
Also hand-woven textiles.*

Frette
799 Madison Avenue
New York, NY 10021
212 988 5221
www.frette.com
*Elegant linens, including
French imports.*

Hancock Fabrics
Visit the website for a retailer
near you.
877 FABRICS
www.hancockfabrics.com
America's largest fabric store.

Hinson & Co.
979 Third Avenue
New York, NY 10022
212 688 5538
*Fabrics, coordinating wall coverings,
and decorative accessories with an
emphasis on clean design.*

Laura Ashley
Check the website for a stockist
near you.
www.lauraashley-usa.com
*Floral, striped, checked, and solid
cotton fabrics in a wide range
of colors.*

Pierre Deux
625 Madison Avenue
New York, NY 10022
212 521 8012
www.pierredeux.com
*Fine French country wallpaper,
fabric, upholstery, and antiques.*

Scalamandré
222 East 59th Street
New York, NY 10022
212 980 3888
www.scalamandre.com
*Restores classic fabrics for historic
houses and sells trims, wallpaper,
textiles, and custom carpets.*

Smith + Noble
800 248 8888
www.smithandnoble.com
*Online store selling custommade
window treatments, slipcovers,
and more.*

Waverly
Visit www.waverly.com for outlets.
*Window treatments, floor coverings,
fabric, and furniture.*

PICTURE CREDITS

All photography by Christopher Drake unless specified otherwise.
Illustrations by Marianne Topham.

Key: **ph=photographer, a=above, b=below, r=right, l=left, c=center.**

1 William Yeoward & Colin Orchard's home in London; 2 Valentina Albini's home in Milan; 3 a house in London, architectural design and procurement by Tyler London Ltd, interior design by William W. Stubbs, IIDA; 4–5 ph Chris Everard/designed by Mullman Seidman Architects; 6–7 Bruce Oldfield's former home in Oxfordshire; 7 Clare Mosley's house in London; 8–9 ph Chris Everard/an apartment in Milan designed by Daniela Micol Wajskol, interior designer; 10 ph Tom Leighton/Keith Varty & Alan Cleaver's apartment in London designed by Jonathan Reed; 11a&b a house designed by artist Angela A'Court, extension and alteration to rear of property by S. I. Robertson at 23 Architecture; 12–13 ph Tom Leighton/Keith Varty & Alan Cleaver's apartment in London designed by Jonathan Reed; 14l ph Andrew Wood/Mary Shaw's Sequana apartment in Paris; 14c a house designed by artist Angela A'Court, extension and alteration to rear of property by S. I. Robertson at 23 Architecture; 14–15 Fay & Roger Oates' house in Ledbury; 15 Maurizio Epifani's home in Milan; 16, 16–17, & 17ar Vivien Lawrence, an interior designer in London (+44 (0)20 8209 0562); 18 ph Alan Williams/the architect Voon Wong's own apartment in London; 19 ph Chris Everard/Freddie Daniells' apartment in London designed by Brookes Stacey Randall; 20l William Yeoward & Colin Orchard's home in London; 20r an apartment in Milan designed by Daniela Micol Wajskol, interior designer; 21 Bruce Oldfield's former home in Oxfordshire; 22–23 Florence Lim's house in London—architecture by Voon Wong Architects, interior design by Florence Lim Design; 24–29 William Yeoward & Colin Orchard's home in London; 30–35 Florence Lim's house in London —architecture by Voon Wong Architects, interior design by Florence Lim Design; 36–41 Bruce Oldfield's former home in Oxfordshire; 42–43 designed by McLean Quinlan Architects; 44cr ph Chris Everard/designed by Mullman Seidman Architects; 46–49 ph Chris Everard/an apartment in Milan designed by Daniela Micol Wajskol, interior designer; 50–53 Fay & Roger Oates' house in Ledbury; 54–57 designed by McLean Quinlan Architects; 58–61 ph Andrew Wood/Mary Shaw's Sequana apartment in Paris; 62–65 Vivien Lawrence, an interior designer in London (+44 (0)20 8209 0562); 66–69 ph Alan Williams/interior designer John Barman's own apartment in New York; 70–73 ph Chris Everard/designed by Mullman Seidman Architects; 76–79 a house in Salisbury designed by Helen Ellery of The Plot London; 80–83 a house in London, architectural design and procurement by Tyler London Ltd, interior design by William W. Stubbs, IIDA; 84–89 a house designed by artist Angela A'Court, extension and alteration to rear of property by S. I. Robertson at 23 Architecture; 90–93 Maurizio Epifani's home in Milan; 94–97 Nordic Style Kitchen; 98–101 Valentina Albini's home in Milan; 104–107 Fay & Roger Oates' house in Ledbury; 108–111 Valentina Albini's home in Milan; 114–117 Clare Mosley's house in London; 118–121 an apartment in Milan designed by Daniela Micol Wajskol, interior designer; 122–125 designed by McLean Quinlan Architects; 126–129 ph Debi Treloar/the Boyes' home in London designed by Circus Architects; 130–133 Nordic Style Bedroom; 136–139 a house in Salisbury designed by Helen Ellery of The Plot London;

BUSINESS CREDITS

Architects and designers whose work has been featured in this book:

Key: **a=above, b=below, r=right, l=left, c=center.**

23 Architecture
S. I. Robertson
318 Kensal Road
London W10 5BZ UK
tel. +44 (0)20 8962 8666
fax. +44 (0)20 8962 8777
stuart@23arc.com
www.23arc.com
Pages 11a&b, 14c, 84–89, 170–171, 173c, 174al, 192.

Angela A'Court
Artist
orangedawe@hotmail.com
Pages 11a&b, 14c, 84–89, 170–171, 173c, 174al, 192.

Nicholas Arbuthnott
Arbuthnott Ladenbury Architects
Architects & Urban Designers
15 Gosditch Street
Cirencester GL7 2AG UK
and
Vanessa Arbuthnott Fabrics
tel. +44 (0)1285 831437
www.vanessaarbuthnott.co.uk
Page 183ar.

John Barman Inc.
Interior design & decoration
500 Park Avenue
New York NY 10022
tel. 212 838 9443
john@barman.com
www.johnbarman.com
Pages 66–69, 175a.

behun/ziff design
153 E. 53rd Street
43rd Floor
New York NY 10022
tel. 212 292 6233
fax. 212 292 6790
Pages 104–143.

Bruce Bierman Design, Inc.
29 West 15th Street
New York NY 10011
tel. 212 243 1935
fax. 212 243 6615
www.biermandesign.com
Page 172a.

Stephen Blatt Architects
10 Danforth Street
Portland ME 04101
tel. 207 761 5911
fax. 207 761 2105
sba@sbarchitects.com
www.sbarchitects.com
Page 173b.

Brookes Stacey Randall
www.bsr-architects.com
Pages 19, 182b.

Circus Architects
7 Brooks Court
Kirtling Street
London SW8 5BP UK
tel. +44 (0)20 7627 6080
contact@circus-architects.com
www.circus-architects.com
Pages 126–129.

Charlotte Crosland Interiors
62 St Mark's Road
London W10 6NN UK
tel. +44 (0)20 8960 9442
fax. +44 (0)20 8960 9714
mail@charlottecrosland.com
www.charlottecrosland.com
Page 181al.

Helen Ellery of The Plot London
77 Compton Street
London EC1V 0BN UK
tel. +44 (0)20 7251 8116
fax. +44 (0)20 7251 8117
helen@theplotlondon.com
www.theplotlondon.com
Pages 76–79, 136–139, 174c, 177al, 177c.

L'oro dei Farlocchi
Via Madonnina 5
20121 Milano
Italy
tel./fax. +39 02 860589
www.lorodeifarlocchi.com
Pages 15, 90–93, 174–175, 183b.

Vivien Lawrence Interior Design
Interior designer of private homes—any project from start to finish. London.
tel. +44 (0)20 8209 0058/8209 0562
fax. +44 (0)20 8209 0562
vl-interiordesign@cwcom.net
Specialist decoration by Annie Le Painter tel. +44 (0)20 7609 6339
Curtains/blinds/soft furnishings by Heads and Tails tel. +44 (0)1559 363868
Pages 16, 16–17, 17ar, 62–65, 175c, 178a&b.

Marino + Giolito
161 West 16th Street
New York NY 10011
tel./fax. 212 675 5737
Pages 162–165.

McLean Quinlan Architects
1 Milliners
Eastfields Avenue
London SW18 1LP UK
tel. +44 (0)20 8870 8600
info@mcleanquinlan.com
www.mcleanquinlan.com
Pages 42–43, 54–57, 122–125, 177b.

David Mikhail Architects
Unit 29, 1–13 Adler Street
London E1 1EE UK
tel. +44 (0)20 7377 8724
info@davidmikhail.com
www.davidmikhail.com
Pages 152–155.

Clare Mosley
Gilding, *eglomise* panels & mirrors, lampbases, finials, & curtain accessories.
tel./fax. +44 (0)20 7708 3123
Pages 7, 114–117, 148–151, 172c.

140–143 ph Chris Everard/the Sugarman–Behun house on Long Island; 144–147 ph Chris Everard/designed by Zynk Design Consultants, One New Inn Square, a private dining room and home of chef David Vanderhook, all enquiries +44 (0)20 7729 3645; 148–151 Clare Mosley's house in London; 152–155 ph Chris Everard/Simon Brignall & Christina Rosetti's loft apartment in London designed by David Mikhail Architects; 156ac ph Andrew Wood; 158–161 an apartment in Milan designed by Daniela Micol Wajskol, interior designer; 162–165 ph Andrew Wood/Chelsea Studio New York City, designed by Marino + Giolito; 166–169 a house in London, architectural design and procurement by Tyler London Ltd, interior design by William W. Stubbs, IIDA; 170–171 a house designed by artist Angela A'Court, extension and alteration to rear of property by S. I. Robertson at 23 Architecture; 172a ph Alan Williams/New York apartment designed by Bruce Bierman; 172c Clare Mosley's house in London; 172b ph Andrew Wood/Mary Shaw's Sequana apartment in Paris; 173al ph Christopher Drake/Mark Wilkinson's farmhouse in Wiltshire; 173ar ph Alan Williams/the architect Voon Wong's own apartment in London; 173c a house designed by artist Angela A'Court, extension and alteration to rear of property by S. I. Robertson at 23 Architecture; 173b ph Jan Baldwin/a house in Cape Elizabeth designed by Stephen Blatt Architects; 174al a house designed by artist Angela A'Court, extension and alteration to rear of property by S. I. Robertson at 23 Architecture; 174c a house in Salisbury designed by Helen Ellery of The Plot London; 174b ph Chris Everard/designed by Zynk Design Consultants, One New Inn Square, a private dining room and home of chef David Vanderhook, all enquiries +44 (0)20 7729 3645; 174–175 Maurizio Epifani's home in Milan; 175a ph Alan Williams/interior designer John Barman's own apartment in New York; 175c Vivien Lawrence, an interior designer in London (+44 (0)20 8209 0562); 175b Fay & Roger Oates' house in Ledbury;

176a Nordic Style Bedroom; 176c ph Ray Main/Darren and Sheila Chadwick's apartment in London designed by Sergisson Bates; 176b Bruce Oldfield's former home in Oxfordshire; 177al&c a house in Salisbury designed by Helen Ellery of The Plot London; 177ar Fay & Roger Oates' house in Ledbury; 177b designed by McLean Quinlan Architects; 178a&b Vivien Lawrence, an interior designer in London (+44 (0)20 8209 0562); 178c ph Jan Baldwin/Constanze von Unruh's house in London; 179al William Yeoward & Colin Orchard's home in London; 179ar Valentina Albini's home in Milan; 179c Nordic Style Kitchen; 179b ph Polly Wreford/Ros Fairman's house in London; 180a Nordic Style Kitchen; 180c ph Alan Williams/Stanley & Nancy Grossman's apartment in New York designed by Jennifer Post Design; 180b ph Polly Wreford/Kimberley Watson's house in London; 181al ph Andrew Wood/ Charlotte Crosland's home in London, designed by Charlotte Crosland Interiors; 181r ph Chris Everard/designed by Zynk Design Consultants, One New Inn Square, a private dining room and home of chef David Vanderhook, all enquiries +44 (0)20 7729 3645; 181c ph Polly Wreford/the Sawmills Studios; 181b Bruce Oldfield's former home in Oxfordshire; 182a ph Alan Williams/Margot Feldman's house in New York designed by Patricia Seidman of Mullman Seidman Architects; 182c ph Jan Baldwin/ Peter & Nicole Dawes' apartment, designed by Mullman Seidman Architects; 182b ph Chris Everard/Freddie Daniells' apartment in London designed by Brookes Stacey Randall; 183al ph Alan Williams/Katie Bassford King's house in London designed by Touch Interior Design; 183ar ph Alan Williams/the Arbuthnott family's house near Cirencester designed by Nicholas Arbuthnott, fabrics designed by Vanessa Arbuthnott; 183c an apartment in Milan designed by Daniela Micol Wajskol, interior designer; 183b Maurizio Epifani's home in Milan; 192 a house designed by artist Angela A'Court, extension and alteration to rear of property by S. I. Robertson at 23 Architecture.

Mullman Seidman Architects
Architecture & interior design
443 Greenwich Street # 2A
New York NY 10013
tel. 212 431 0770
fax. 212 431 8428
msa@mullmanseidman.com
www.mullmanseidman.com
Pages 4–5, 44cr, 70–73, 182a, 182c.

Nordic Style
Classic Swedish interiors
109 Lots Road
London SW10 0RN UK
tel. +44 (0)20 7351 1755
fax. +44 (0)20 7351 4966
www.nordicstyle.com
Pages 94–97, 130–133, 176a, 179c, 180a.

Roger Oates Design
tel. +44 (0)1531 632718
www.rogeroates.co.uk
Showrooms:
1 Munro Terrace
Chelsea
London SW10 0DL UK
and
The Long Barn, Eastnor
Herefordshire HR8 1EL UK
Pages 14–15, 50–53, 104–107, 175b, 177ar.

Bruce Oldfield Ltd.
27 Beauchamp Place
London SW3 1NJ UK
tel. +44 (0)20 7584 1363
www.bruceoldfield.com
Pages 6–7, 21, 36–41, 176b, 181b.

Colin Orchard Consultants
219a Kings Road
London SW3 5EJ UK
tel. +44 (0)20 7352 2116
info@colinorchard.com
Pages 1, 20l, 24–29, 179al.

Jennifer Post Design
Spatial & interior designer
25 East 67th Street, 8D
New York NY 10021
tel. 212 734 7994
fax. 212 396 2450
www.jenniferpostdesign.com
Page 180c.

Jonathan Reed
Studio Reed
151a Sydney Street
London SW3 6NT UK
tel. +44 (0)20 7565 0066
fax. +44 (0)20 7565 0067
Pages 10, 12–13.

Sequana
64 Avenue de la Motte Picquet
75015 Paris
France
tel. +33 1 45 66 58 40
fax. +33 1 45 67 99 81
sequana@wanadoo.fr
Page 14l, 58–61, 172b.

Sergission Bates
44 Newman Street
London W1P 3PA UK
tel. +44 (0)20 7255 1564
fax. +44 (0)20 7636 5646
Page 176c.

William W. Stubbs, IIDA
William W. Stubbs and Associates
2100 Tanglewilde, Suite 17
Houston TX 77063
stubbsww1@aol.com
Pages 3, 80–83, 166–169.

Touch Interior Design
tel. +44 (0)20 7498 6409
Page 183al

Tyler London Ltd.
22a Ives Street
London SW3 2ND UK
tel. +44 (0)20 7581 3677
fax. +44 (0)20 7581 8115
www.tylerlondon.com
Pages 3, 80–83, 166–169.

Constanze von Unruh
Constanze Interior Projects
Interior design company
Richmond
Surrey UK
tel. +44 (0)20 8948 5533
constanze@constanzeinteriorprojects.com
Page 178c.

David Vanderhook
tel. +44 (0)20 7729 3645
Pages 144–147, 174b, 181r.

Daniela Micol Wajskol
Interior designer
Via Vincenzo Monti 42
20123 Milano
Italy
daniela.w@tiscalinet.it
Pages 8–9, 20r, 46–49, 118–121, 158–161, 183c.

Mark Wilkinson Furniture Ltd.
Beautifully designed and crafted English fitted furniture.
Overton House
High Street
Bromham
Nr. Chippenham
Wiltshire SN15 2HA UK
tel. +44 (0)1380 850004
fax. +44 (0)1380 850184
inquiries@mwf.com
www.mwf.com
Page 173al.

Voon Wong & Benson Saw
(formerly Voon Wong Architects)
Unit 3D
Burbage House
83 Curtain Road
London EC2A 3BS UK
tel. +44 (0)20 7033 8763
info@voon-benson.com
www.voon-benson.com
Pages 18 22–23, 30–35, 173ar.

William Yeoward
270 Kings Road
London SW3 5AW UK
tel. +44 (0)20 7349 7828
www.williamyeoward.com
Pages 1, 20l, 24–29, 179al.

Zynk Design Consultants
11 The Chandlery
50 Westminster Bridge Road
London SE1 7QY UK
tel. +44 (0)20 7721 7444
fax. +44 (0)20 7721 7443
www.zynkdesign.com
Pages 144–147, 174b, 181r.

INDEX